MY WAR WITH BRIAN

Ted Rall, 37, is an award-winning political and social-commentary cartoonist for Universal Press Syndicate. His cartoons appear in the New York Times, Washington Post, Los Angeles Times, San Francisco Examiner, Baltimore Sun and more than 100 other publications. His editorial cartoons won the 1995 Robert F. Kennedy Journalism Award and in 1996 he was a finalist for the Pulitzer Prize. His first book for NBM, Real Americans Admit: The Worst Thing I've Ever Done!, won the 1997 Firecracker Alternative Book Award in the graphic novel category.

Also available by Ted Rall from NBM:
Real Americans Admit: The Worst Thing I've Ever Done!, $8.95
(Add $3 P&H 1st item, $1 each addt'l.)

Other books by Rall:
Waking Up In America (St. Martin's Press), 1992
All The Rules Have Changed (Rip Off Press), 1995
Revenge of the Latchkey Kids (Workman Publishing), 1998

My War With Brian is dedicated to the loners, misfits and losers for whom childhood is an unspeakable horror. Hang tough—adulthood really is better.
Bucketloads of thanks go to my wife Judy, who did all of the pattern shading in this book, and to Terry Nantier at NBM, for having the balls to publish it.

We have over 150 graphic novels in print, write for our color catalog:
NBM
555 8th Ave. Suite 1202
New York, NY 10018
www.nbmpublishing.com

ISBN 1-56163-215-5
©1998 by Ted Rall

5   4   3   2

ComicsLit is an imprint and trademark of:

NANTIER · BEALL · MINOUSTCHINE
Publishing inc.
new york

MY WAR WITH BRIAN

BY TED RALL

NBM
ComicsLit

INTRODUCTION
by Ted Rall

I spent the summer of '79 hanging out with Bill Taylor, an underachieving computer geek who ran the commissary at Woodland Trails Boy Scout Camp, an unassuming patch of forest in southwestern Ohio. Neither of us had very much to do -as far as I could tell, my duties as a camp counselor were strictly optional- and that suited us both just fine.

Like me, Bill had a dark sense of humor, and we shared the same taste in music. (Inexplicably, he liked Jethro Tull and the Boomtown Rats, though.) He had trouble with bullies, but his biggest problem in life was his father. Dad was a Protestant minister, and he insisted that Bill follow in his footsteps. Unfortunately, Bill thought religion was horseshit, and shared these feelings with his father frequently. His dad wouldn't budge, however, and Bill knew that he was doomed to a life in the clergy. Bill and I both went to Fairmont West High School, but we weren't in any of the same classes so we didn't see each other much. A few weeks into the first term, I ran into him in the hallway.

"Hey, what's up?" I asked him.

"Nothing much," he replied, "except that I'm going to kill myself."

"Yeah, I know what you mean," I said, not having the foggiest idea what he meant. Bill disappeared into the swarm of students making their way to class through the West Unit hallways, and I never saw him again. Three days later, his parents discovered him hanging from a Radio Shack stereo cord in the basement of their three-bedroom house. The next afternoon I found his letter in my mailbox; he'd mailed it just two days earlier. "Dear Ted," the letter began, "Don't blame yourself. You were my only friend."

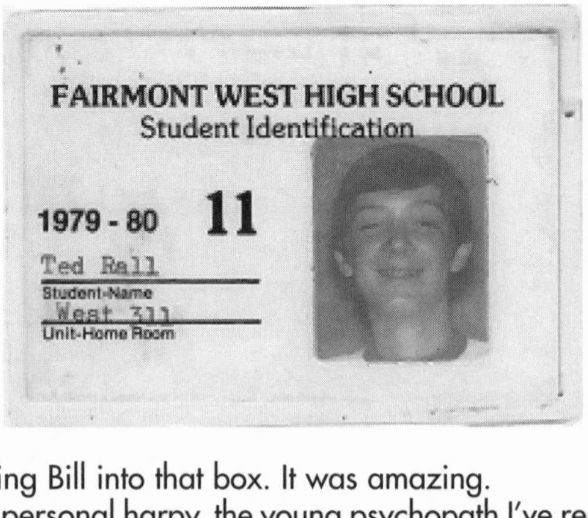
FAIRMONT WEST HIGH SCHOOL
Student Identification
1979 - 80
11
Ted Rall
Student Name
West 311
Unit-Home Room

At the funeral I ran into several of the guys who used to beat up Bill. Anything to score a day off from school, I guess, or perhaps they were too thick to grasp the extent to which they had contributed to putting Bill into that box. It was amazing.

By then I had triumphed over my own personal harpy, the young psychopath I've renamed Brian Koff for the purpose of the following story. But I remained permanently scarred by the realization that nobody really gives a shit about anybody else. My classmates were perhaps too immature to stand up for me -though I doubt that. Maybe my teachers were unaware of the extent of the torment I endured- though I doubt that, too. I know that my mom cared deeply, but she was in no position to help. In the end, I discovered, you're always on your own.

Most people accept that harsh reality at some point, and it changes them. They get hard, even preemptively mean. They lose their humanity in their struggle to survive. But a few, like Bill, decide not to capitulate to the everyday lunacy. They remain true to themselves by opting out of a society unworthy of the word. Bill chose decency, but I wish he'd chosen expedience instead.

-1-
SUBURB OF THE DAMNED

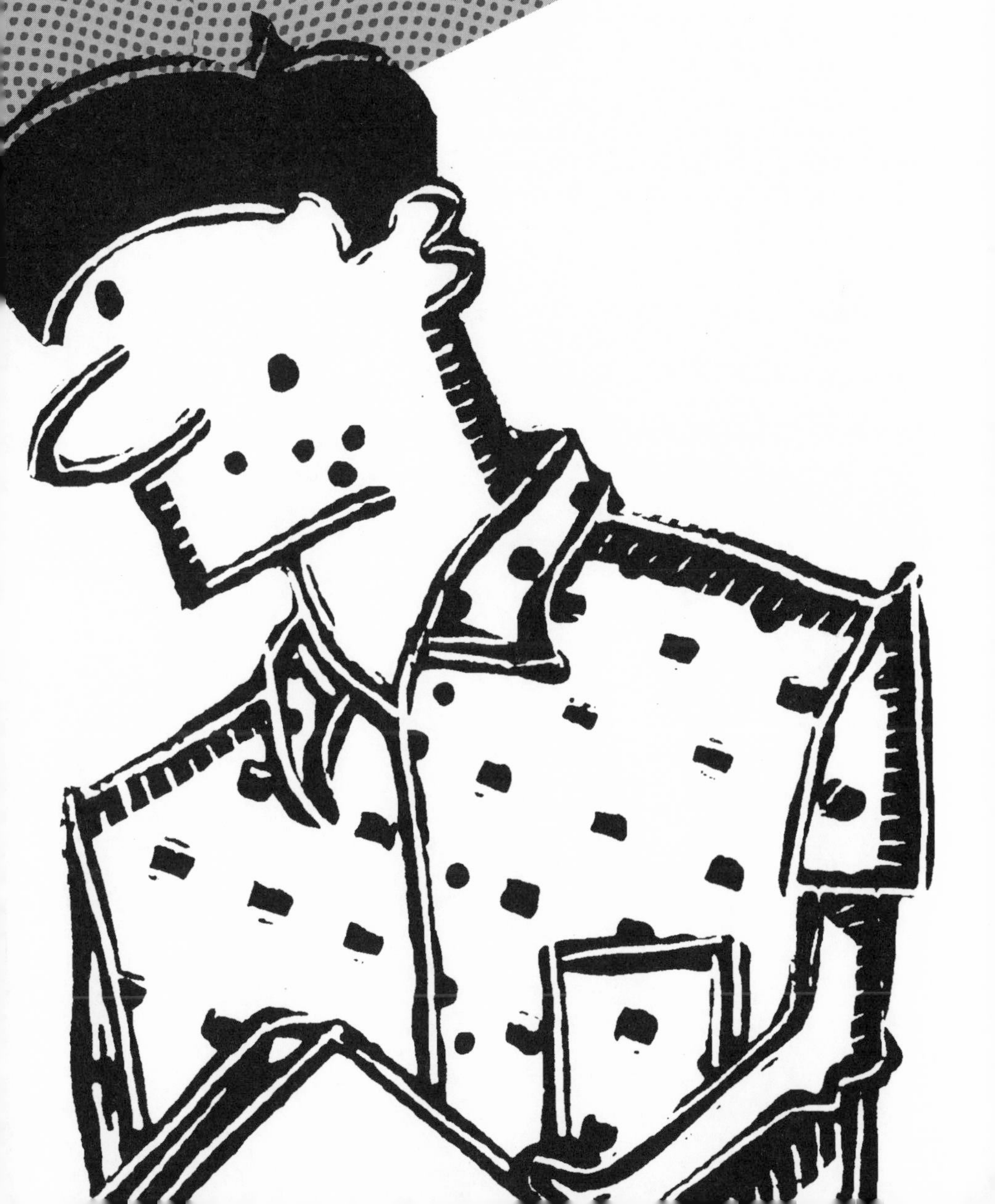

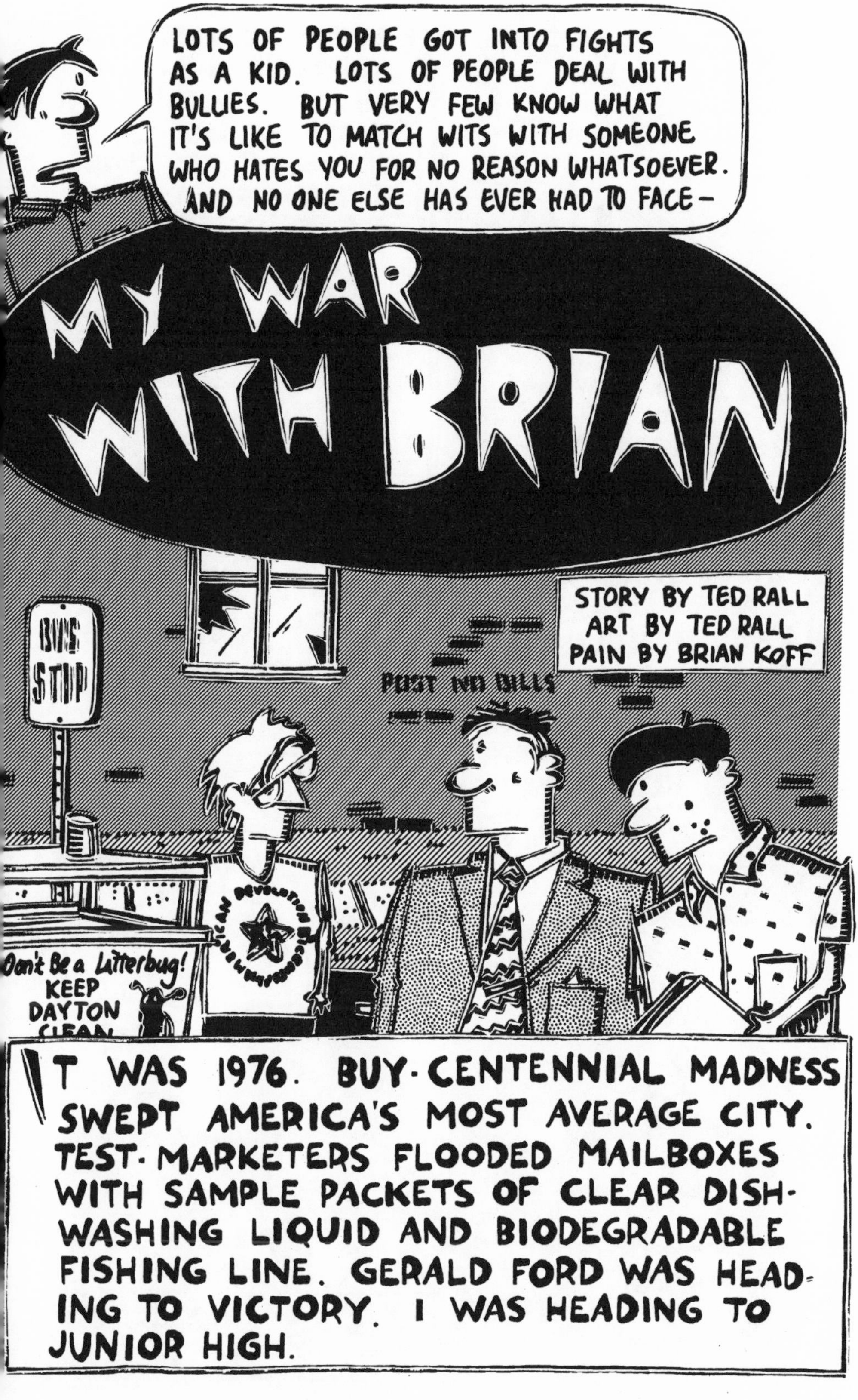
LOTS OF PEOPLE GOT INTO FIGHTS AS A KID. LOTS OF PEOPLE DEAL WITH BULLIES. BUT VERY FEW KNOW WHAT IT'S LIKE TO MATCH WITS WITH SOMEONE WHO HATES YOU FOR NO REASON WHATSOEVER. AND NO ONE ELSE HAS EVER HAD TO FACE—
MY WAR WITH BRIAN
STORY BY TED RALL
ART BY TED RALL
PAIN BY BRIAN KOFF
BUS STOP
POST NO BILLS
Don't Be a Litterbug! KEEP DAYTON
IT WAS 1976. BUY-CENTENNIAL MADNESS SWEPT AMERICA'S MOST AVERAGE CITY. TEST-MARKETERS FLOODED MAILBOXES WITH SAMPLE PACKETS OF CLEAR DISH-WASHING LIQUID AND BIODEGRADABLE FISHING LINE. GERALD FORD WAS HEAD-ING TO VICTORY. I WAS HEADING TO JUNIOR HIGH.

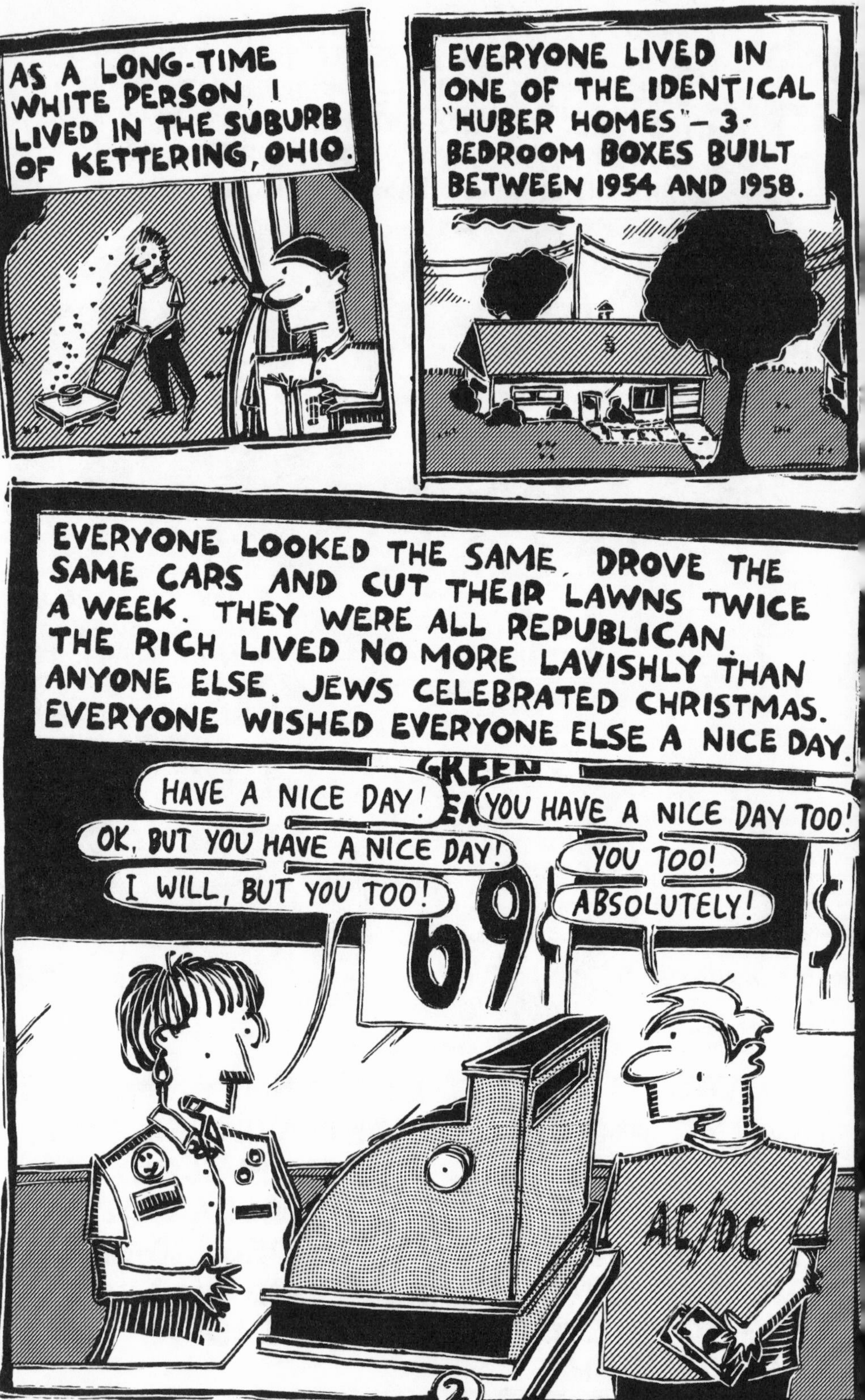
AS A LONG-TIME WHITE PERSON, I LIVED IN THE SUBURB OF KETTERING, OHIO.
EVERYONE LIVED IN ONE OF THE IDENTICAL "HUBER HOMES" – 3-BEDROOM BOXES BUILT BETWEEN 1954 AND 1958.
EVERYONE LOOKED THE SAME, DROVE THE SAME CARS AND CUT THEIR LAWNS TWICE A WEEK. THEY WERE ALL REPUBLICAN. THE RICH LIVED NO MORE LAVISHLY THAN ANYONE ELSE. JEWS CELEBRATED CHRISTMAS. EVERYONE WISHED EVERYONE ELSE A NICE DAY.
HAVE A NICE DAY!
YOU HAVE A NICE DAY TOO!
OK, BUT YOU HAVE A NICE DAY!
YOU TOO!
I WILL, BUT YOU TOO!
ABSOLUTELY!
69
AC/DC

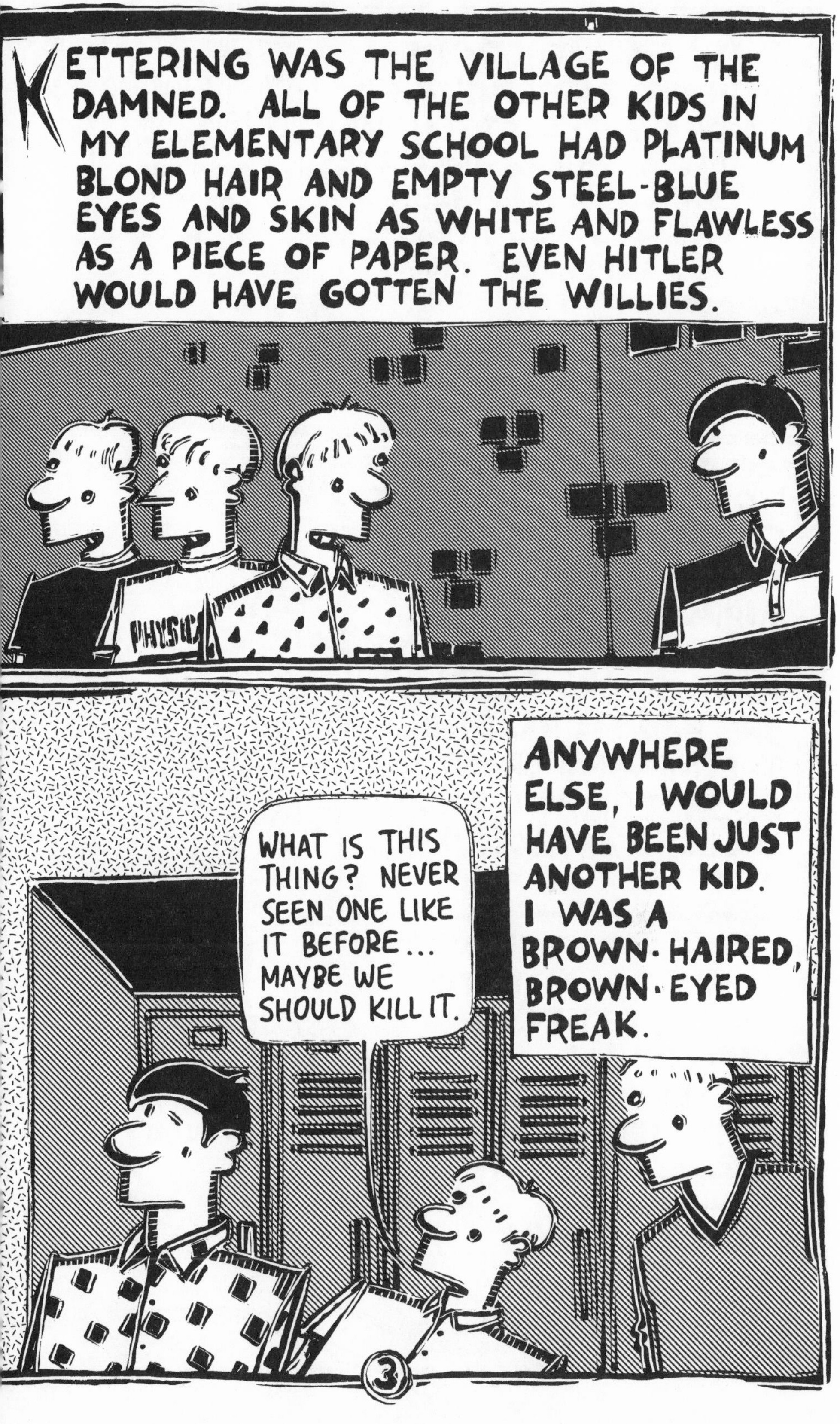
KETTERING WAS THE VILLAGE OF THE DAMNED. ALL OF THE OTHER KIDS IN MY ELEMENTARY SCHOOL HAD PLATINUM BLOND HAIR AND EMPTY STEEL-BLUE EYES AND SKIN AS WHITE AND FLAWLESS AS A PIECE OF PAPER. EVEN HITLER WOULD HAVE GOTTEN THE WILLIES.
PHYSIC
WHAT IS THIS THING? NEVER SEEN ONE LIKE IT BEFORE... MAYBE WE SHOULD KILL IT.
ANYWHERE ELSE, I WOULD HAVE BEEN JUST ANOTHER KID. I WAS A BROWN-HAIRED, BROWN-EYED FREAK.

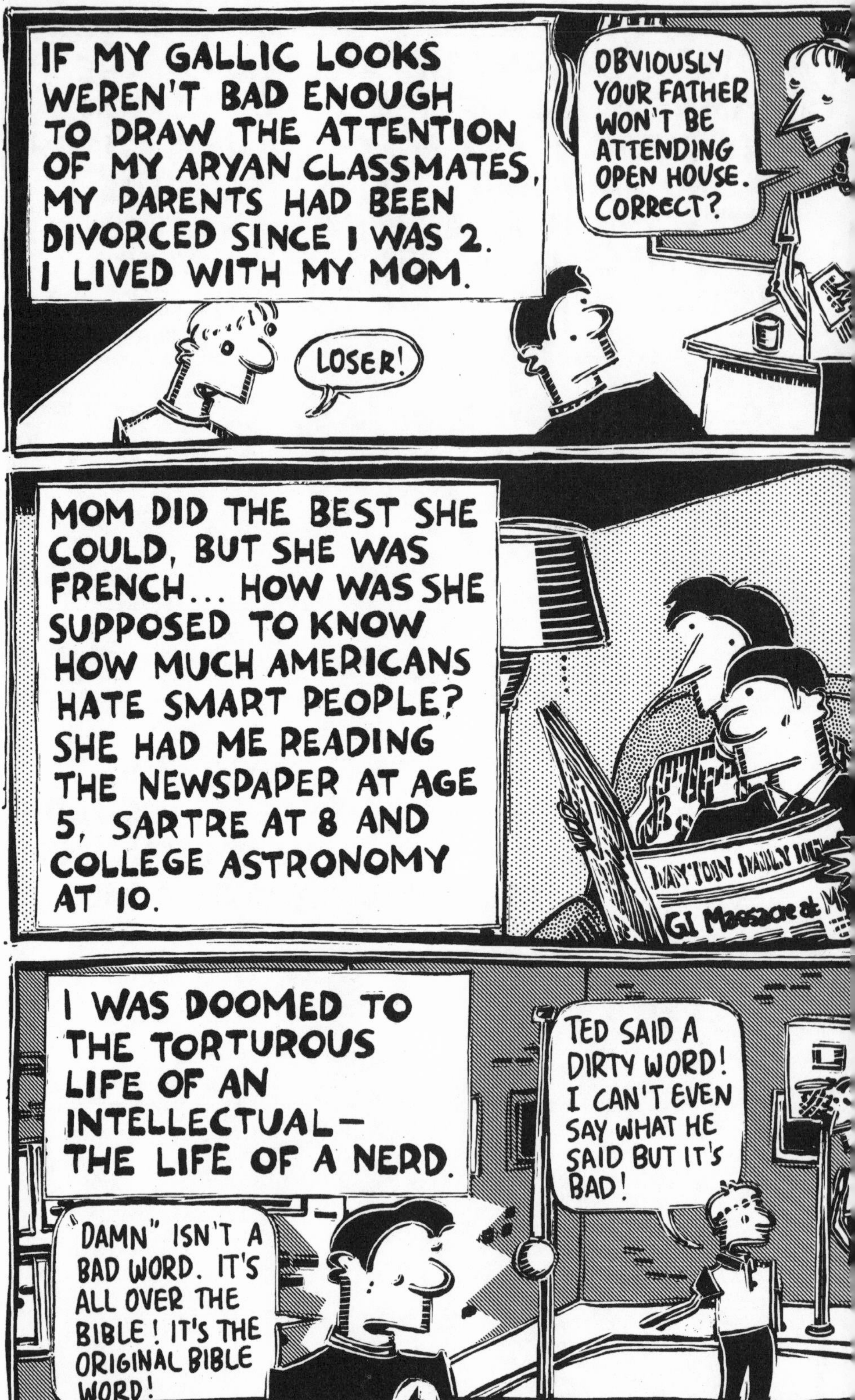
IF MY GALLIC LOOKS WEREN'T BAD ENOUGH TO DRAW THE ATTENTION OF MY ARYAN CLASSMATES, MY PARENTS HAD BEEN DIVORCED SINCE I WAS 2. I LIVED WITH MY MOM.
OBVIOUSLY YOUR FATHER WON'T BE ATTENDING OPEN HOUSE. CORRECT?
LOSER!
MOM DID THE BEST SHE COULD, BUT SHE WAS FRENCH... HOW WAS SHE SUPPOSED TO KNOW HOW MUCH AMERICANS HATE SMART PEOPLE? SHE HAD ME READING THE NEWSPAPER AT AGE 5, SARTRE AT 8 AND COLLEGE ASTRONOMY AT 10.
GI Massacre at
I WAS DOOMED TO THE TORTUROUS LIFE OF AN INTELLECTUAL— THE LIFE OF A NERD.
TED SAID A DIRTY WORD! I CAN'T EVEN SAY WHAT HE SAID BUT IT'S BAD!
"DAMN" ISN'T A BAD WORD. IT'S ALL OVER THE BIBLE! IT'S THE ORIGINAL BIBLE WORD!

-2-
SOMETHING HERE IS NOT LIKE THE OTHER

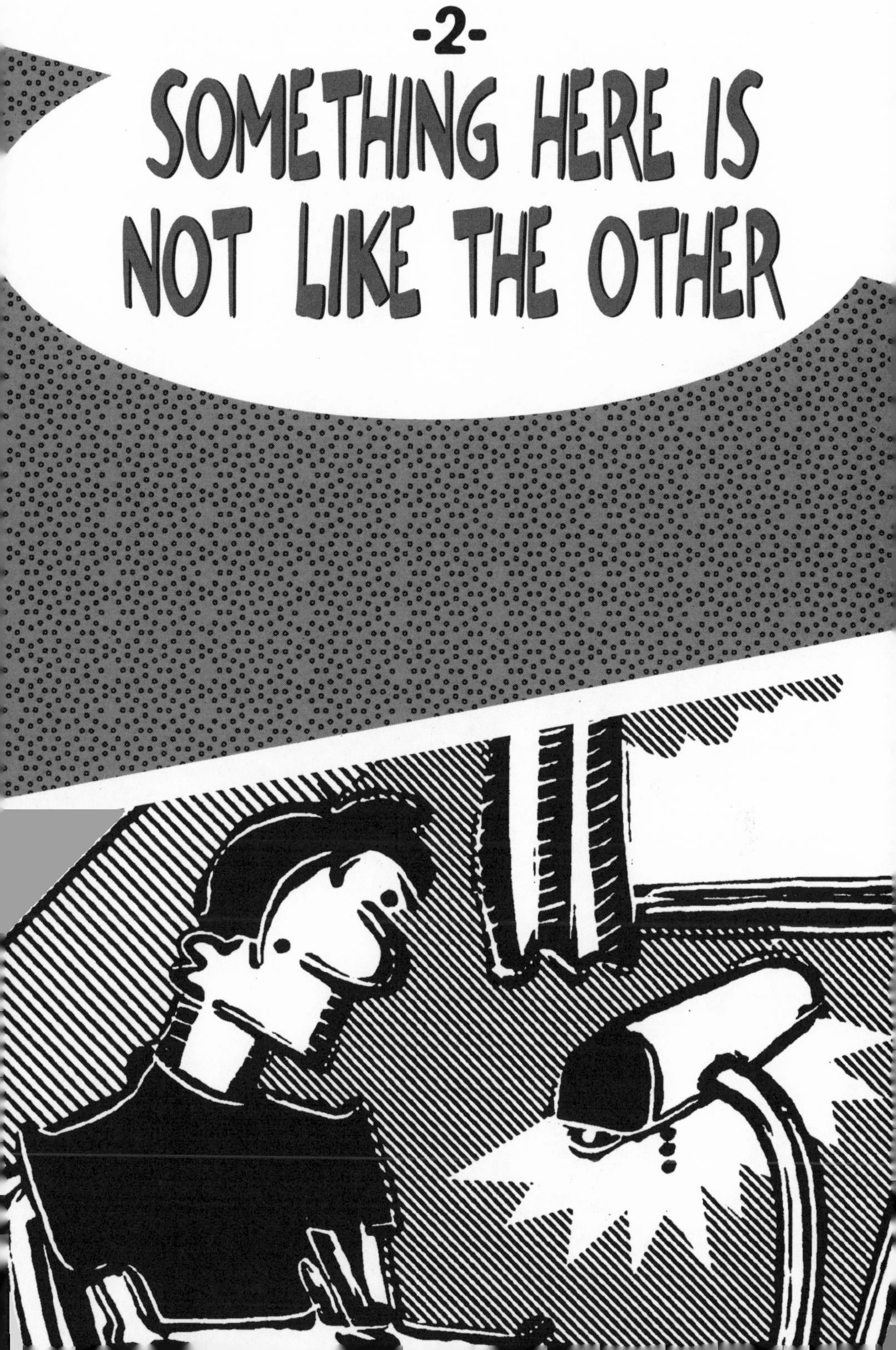

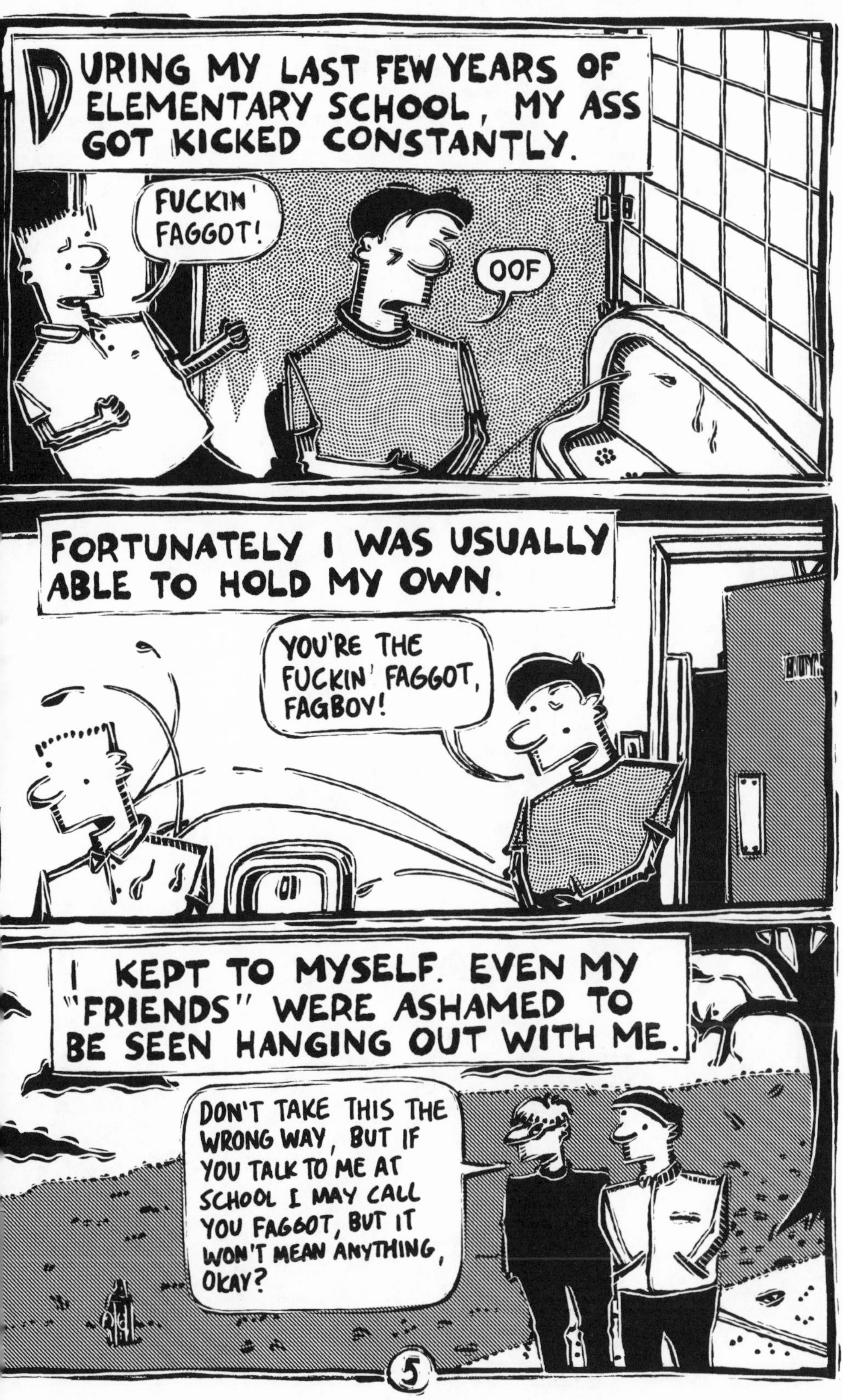
DURING MY LAST FEW YEARS OF ELEMENTARY SCHOOL, MY ASS GOT KICKED CONSTANTLY.
FUCKIN' FAGGOT!
OOF
FORTUNATELY I WAS USUALLY ABLE TO HOLD MY OWN.
YOU'RE THE FUCKIN' FAGGOT, FAGBOY!
I KEPT TO MYSELF. EVEN MY "FRIENDS" WERE ASHAMED TO BE SEEN HANGING OUT WITH ME.
DON'T TAKE THIS THE WRONG WAY, BUT IF YOU TALK TO ME AT SCHOOL I MAY CALL YOU FAGGOT, BUT IT WON'T MEAN ANYTHING, OKAY?

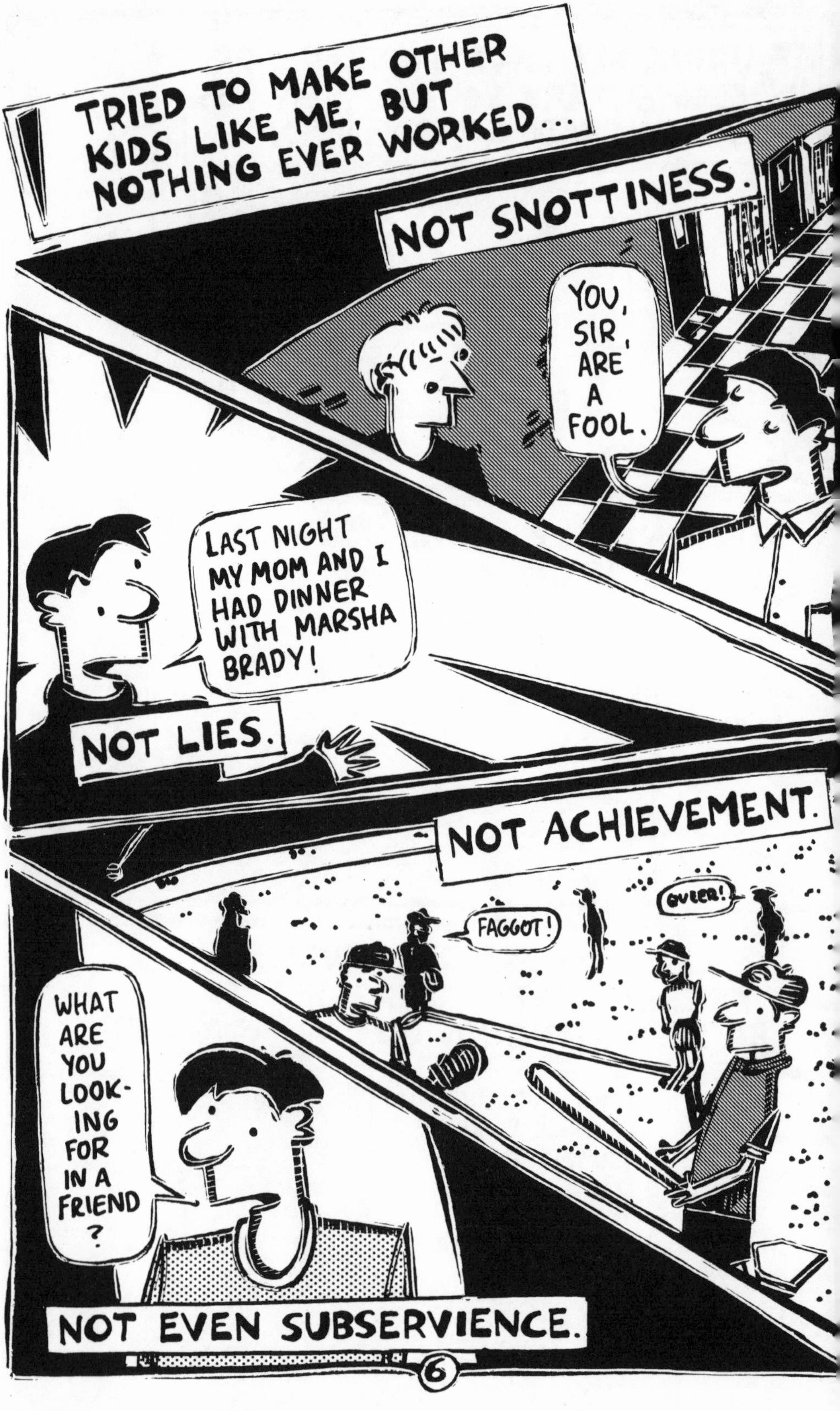

I TRIED TO MAKE OTHER KIDS LIKE ME, BUT NOTHING EVER WORKED...
NOT SNOTTINESS.
YOU, SIR, ARE A FOOL.
LAST NIGHT MY MOM AND I HAD DINNER WITH MARSHA BRADY!
NOT LIES.
NOT ACHIEVEMENT.
FAGGOT!
QUEER!
WHAT ARE YOU LOOK-ING FOR IN A FRIEND ?
NOT EVEN SUBSERVIENCE.

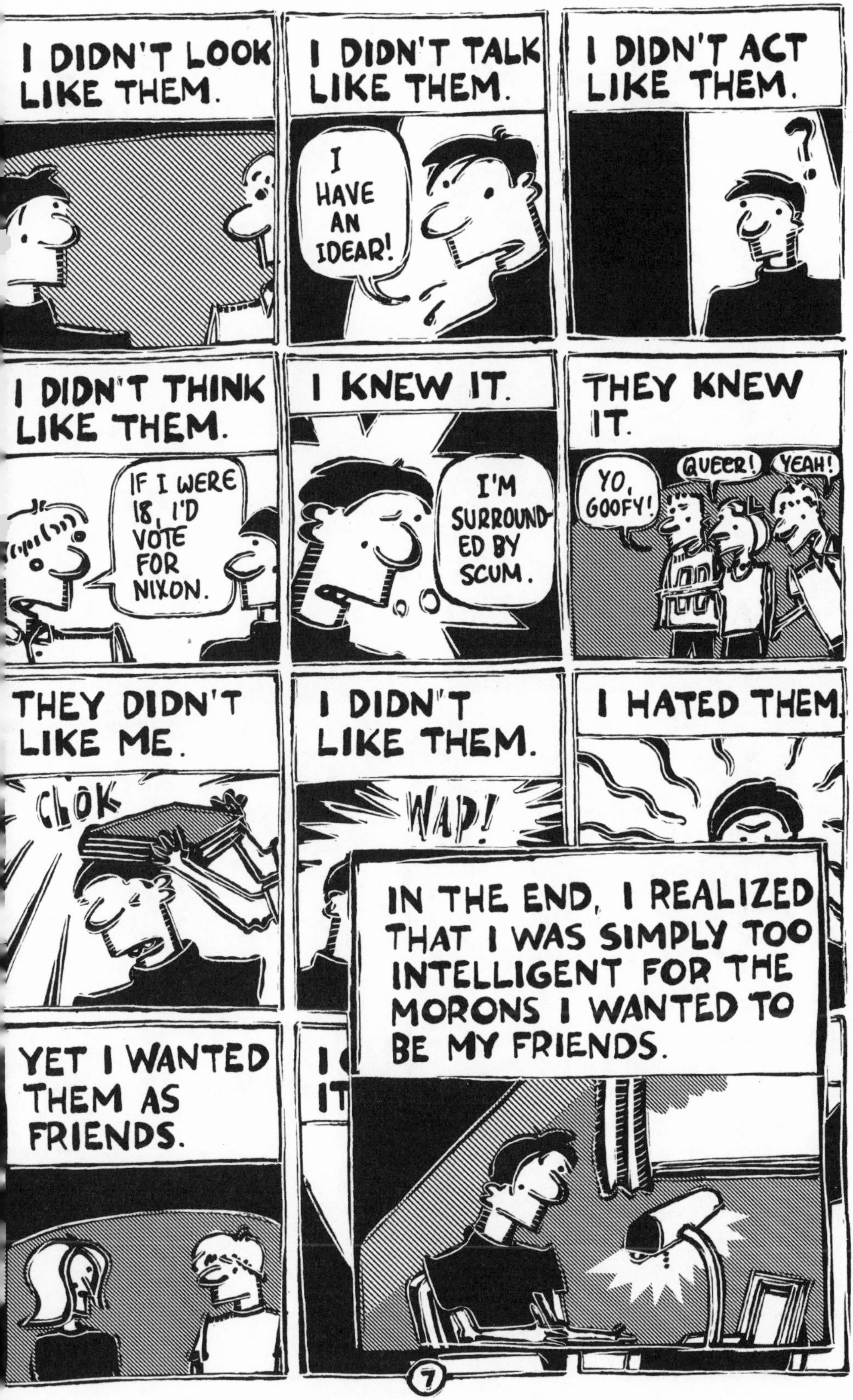

I DIDN'T LOOK LIKE THEM.
I DIDN'T TALK LIKE THEM.
I HAVE AN IDEAR!
I DIDN'T ACT LIKE THEM.
?
I DIDN'T THINK LIKE THEM.
IF I WERE 18, I'D VOTE FOR NIXON.
I KNEW IT.
I'M SURROUNDED BY SCUM.
THEY KNEW IT.
YO, GOOFY!
QUEER!
YEAH!
THEY DIDN'T LIKE ME.
CLOK
I DIDN'T LIKE THEM.
WAP!
I HATED THEM.
YET I WANTED THEM AS FRIENDS.
IN THE END, I REALIZED THAT I WAS SIMPLY TOO INTELLIGENT FOR THE MORONS I WANTED TO BE MY FRIENDS.

Of course I knew that junior high school would be different... seven teachers instead of one... four elementary schools feeding into one junior high... half the kids crazy with puberty and twice as big as the rest of us.

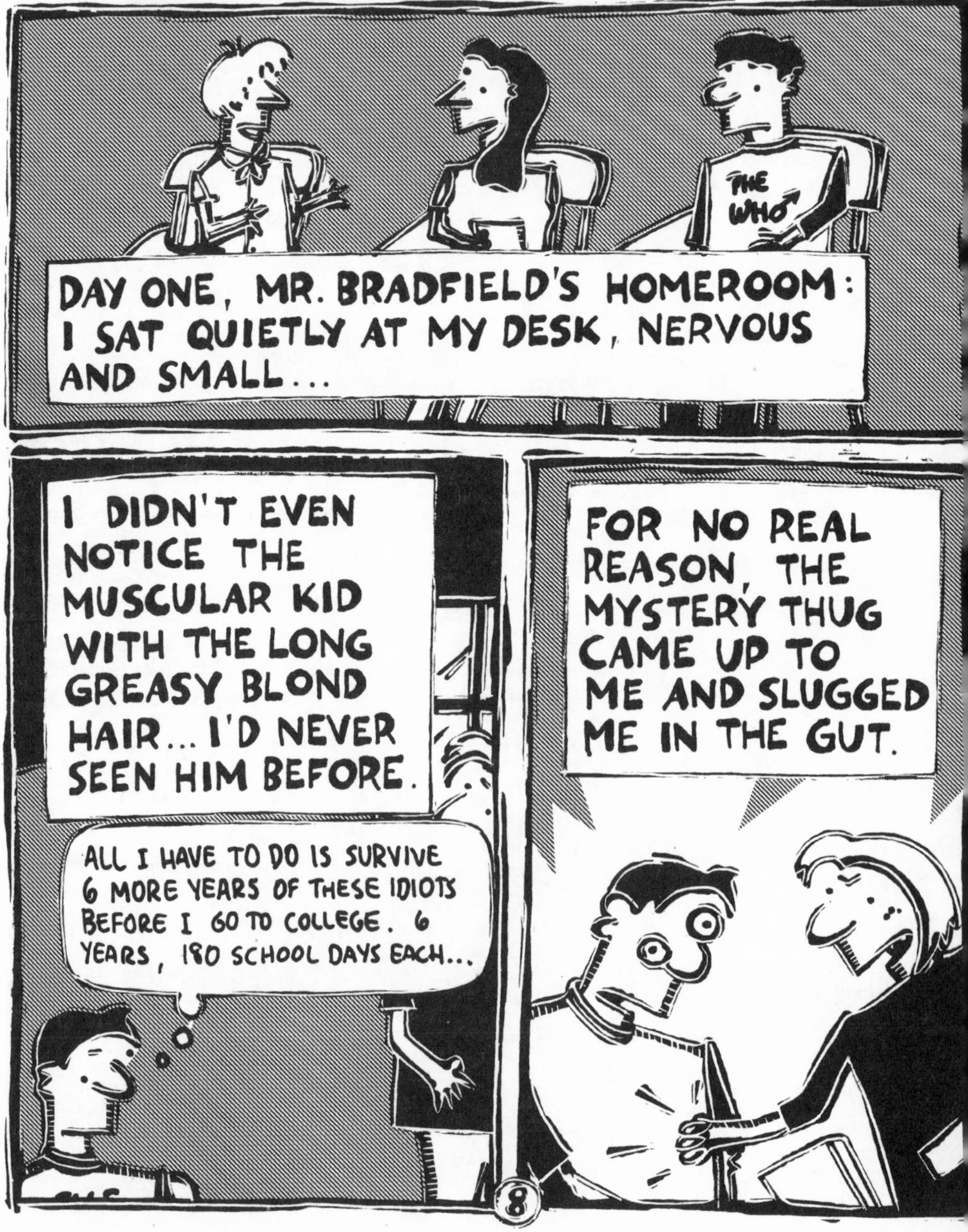
THE WHO
DAY ONE, MR. BRADFIELD'S HOMEROOM: I SAT QUIETLY AT MY DESK, NERVOUS AND SMALL...
I DIDN'T EVEN NOTICE THE MUSCULAR KID WITH THE LONG GREASY BLOND HAIR... I'D NEVER SEEN HIM BEFORE.
ALL I HAVE TO DO IS SURVIVE 6 MORE YEARS OF THESE IDIOTS BEFORE I GO TO COLLEGE. 6 YEARS, 180 SCHOOL DAYS EACH...
FOR NO REAL REASON, THE MYSTERY THUG CAME UP TO ME AND SLUGGED ME IN THE GUT.

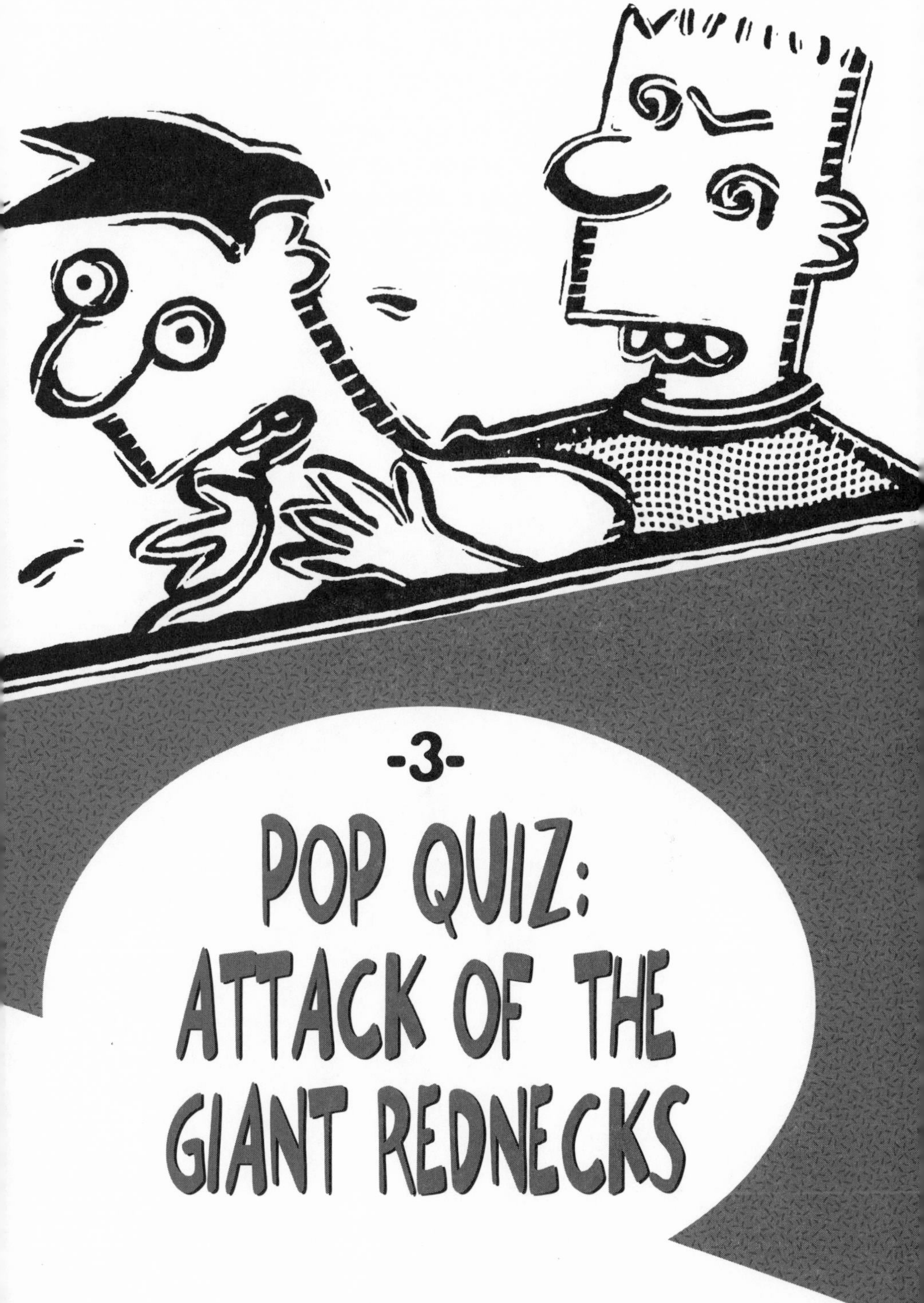

-3-

POP QUIZ: ATTACK OF THE GIANT REDNECKS

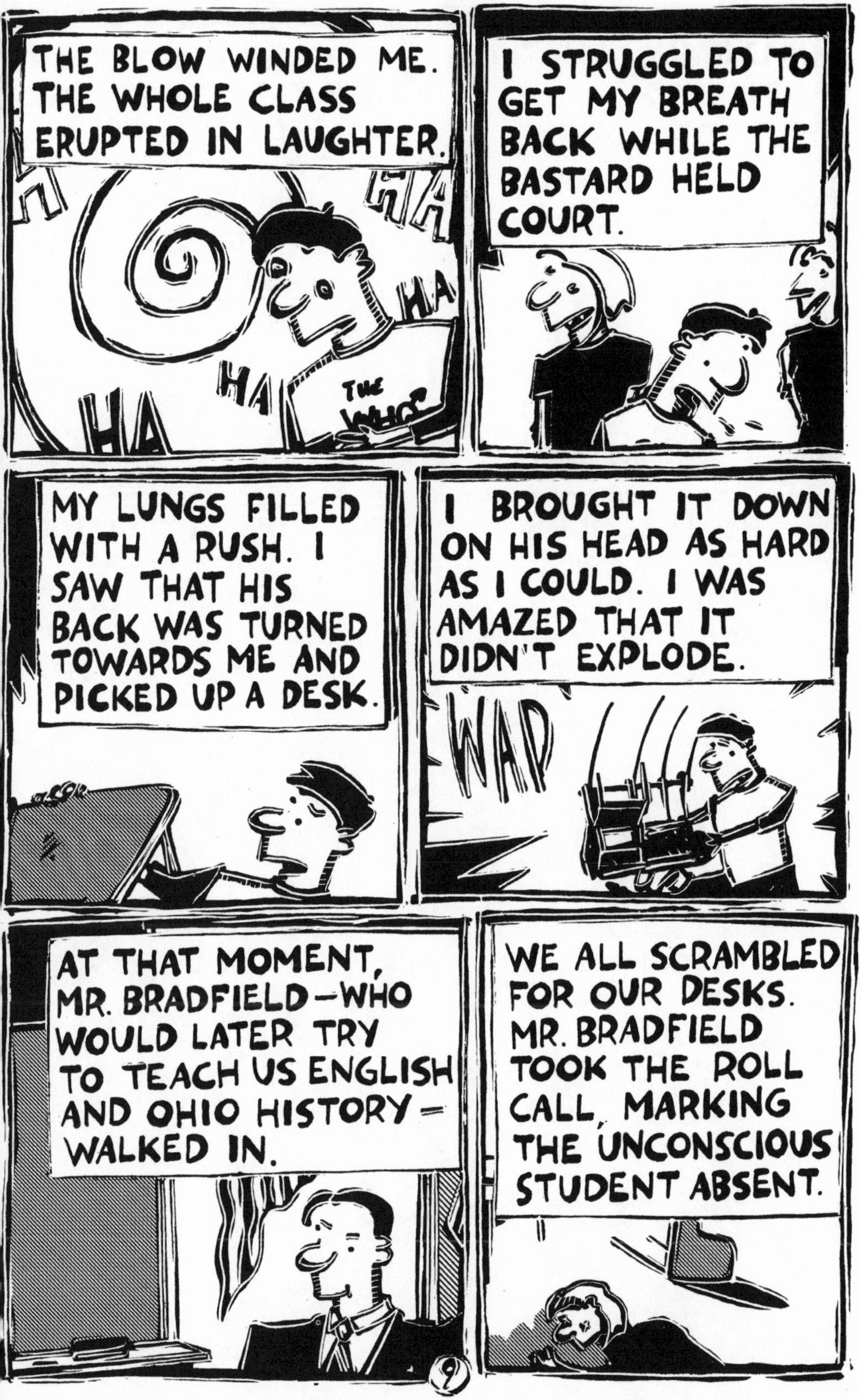
THE BLOW WINDED ME. THE WHOLE CLASS ERUPTED IN LAUGHTER.
HA
HA
HA
HA
I STRUGGLED TO GET MY BREATH BACK WHILE THE BASTARD HELD COURT.
MY LUNGS FILLED WITH A RUSH. I SAW THAT HIS BACK WAS TURNED TOWARDS ME AND PICKED UP A DESK.
I BROUGHT IT DOWN ON HIS HEAD AS HARD AS I COULD. I WAS AMAZED THAT IT DIDN'T EXPLODE.
WAP
AT THAT MOMENT, MR. BRADFIELD—WHO WOULD LATER TRY TO TEACH US ENGLISH AND OHIO HISTORY—WALKED IN.
WE ALL SCRAMBLED FOR OUR DESKS. MR. BRADFIELD TOOK THE ROLL CALL, MARKING THE UNCONSCIOUS STUDENT ABSENT.

AMAZINGLY, NOTHING HAPPENED.

DID YOU SEE THAT?!

IT WAS COOL, MAN!

I KNEW RIGHT THERE AND THEN THAT I WAS ON MY OWN. I'D ENTERED A DARWINIAN NIGHTMARE OF BENIGN NEGLECT.

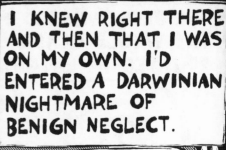

BRADFIELD HERE. PLEASE SEND A NURSE FOR AN UNCONSCIOUS STUDENT.

THE TEACHERS DIDN'T CARE ABOUT THE CONSTANT VIOLENCE.

I DON'T CARE WHO STARTED IT... YOU'RE BOTH ON DETENTION.

THE ADMINISTRATION DIDN'T CARE ABOUT THE ATMOSPHERE OF TERROR.

BOYS'LL BE BOYS!

THE COMMUNITY DIDN'T CARE ABOUT CHILDREN.

YOU BRATS ARE KILLING MY LAWN! GET OUT OR I'LL CALL THE POLICE!

HELP

THEY SAID:

YOU CAN'T ALWAYS GO RUNNING FOR HELP WHEN YOU HAVE A PROBLEM... YOU HAVE TO HANDLE IT YOURSELF!

SO WE DID.

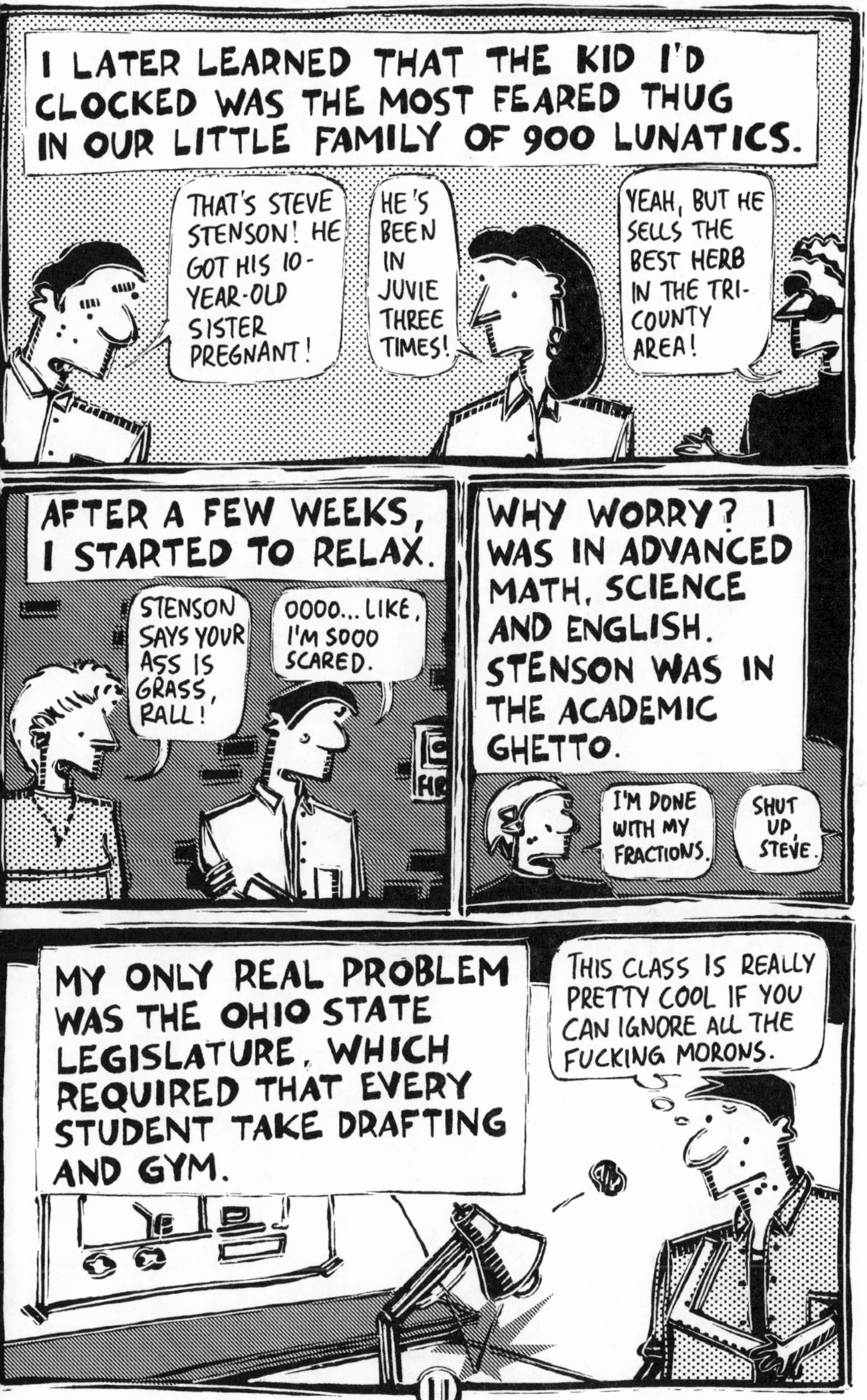
I LATER LEARNED THAT THE KID I'D CLOCKED WAS THE MOST FEARED THUG IN OUR LITTLE FAMILY OF 900 LUNATICS.
THAT'S STEVE STENSON! HE GOT HIS 10-YEAR-OLD SISTER PREGNANT!
HE'S BEEN IN JUVIE THREE TIMES!
YEAH, BUT HE SELLS THE BEST HERB IN THE TRI-COUNTY AREA!
AFTER A FEW WEEKS, I STARTED TO RELAX.
STENSON SAYS YOUR ASS IS GRASS, RALL!
OOOO... LIKE, I'M SOOO SCARED.
WHY WORRY? I WAS IN ADVANCED MATH, SCIENCE AND ENGLISH. STENSON WAS IN THE ACADEMIC GHETTO.
I'M DONE WITH MY FRACTIONS.
SHUT UP, STEVE.
MY ONLY REAL PROBLEM WAS THE OHIO STATE LEGISLATURE, WHICH REQUIRED THAT EVERY STUDENT TAKE DRAFTING AND GYM.
THIS CLASS IS REALLY PRETTY COOL IF YOU CAN IGNORE ALL THE FUCKING MORONS.

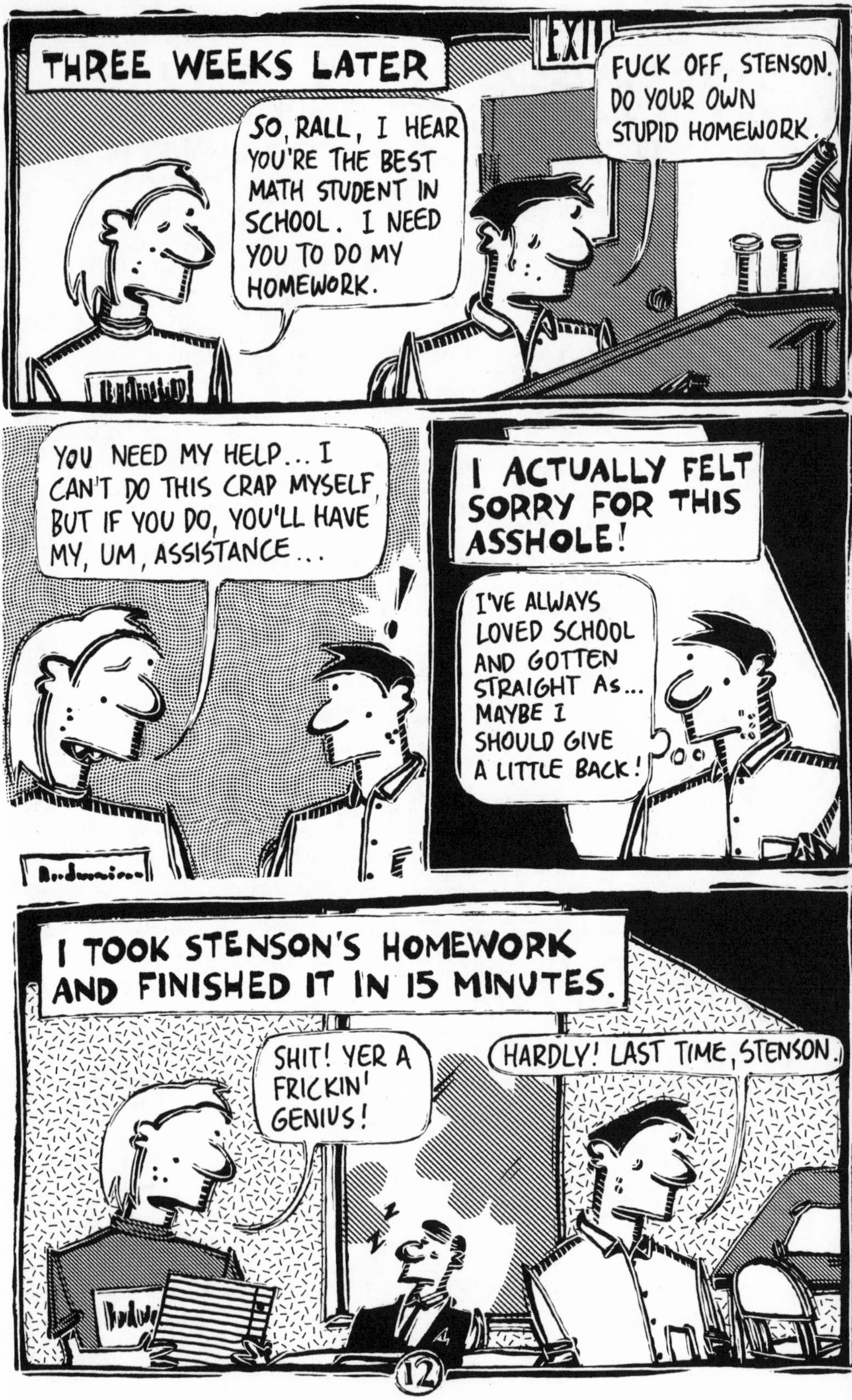
THREE WEEKS LATER
SO, RALL, I HEAR YOU'RE THE BEST MATH STUDENT IN SCHOOL. I NEED YOU TO DO MY HOMEWORK.
FUCK OFF, STENSON. DO YOUR OWN STUPID HOMEWORK.
EXIT
YOU NEED MY HELP... I CAN'T DO THIS CRAP MYSELF, BUT IF YOU DO, YOU'LL HAVE MY, UM, ASSISTANCE...
!
I ACTUALLY FELT SORRY FOR THIS ASSHOLE!
I'VE ALWAYS LOVED SCHOOL AND GOTTEN STRAIGHT As... MAYBE I SHOULD GIVE A LITTLE BACK!
I TOOK STENSON'S HOMEWORK AND FINISHED IT IN 15 MINUTES.
SHIT! YER A FRICKIN' GENIUS!
HARDLY! LAST TIME, STENSON.
Z Z

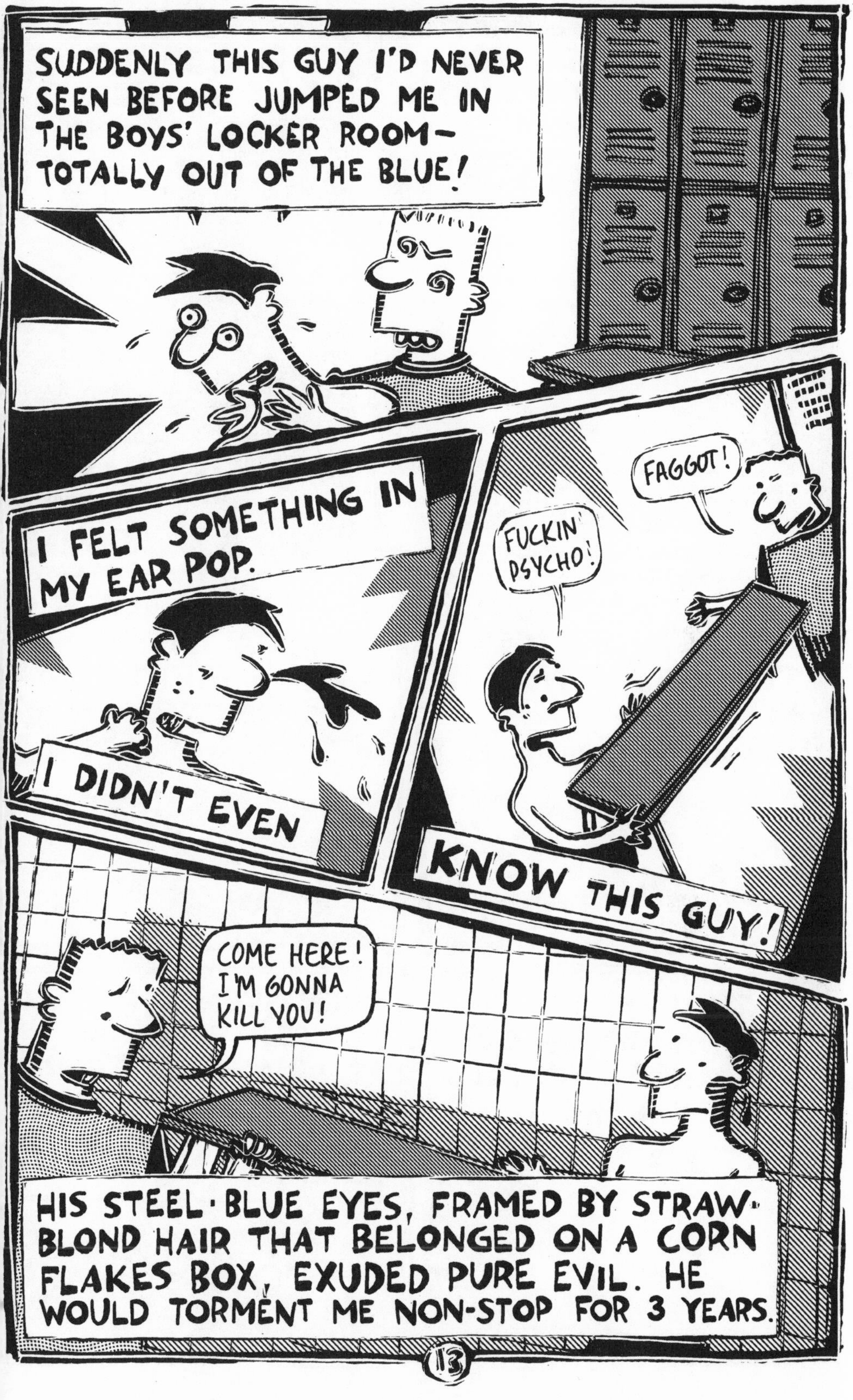

SUDDENLY THIS GUY I'D NEVER SEEN BEFORE JUMPED ME IN THE BOYS' LOCKER ROOM— TOTALLY OUT OF THE BLUE!
I FELT SOMETHING IN MY EAR POP.
I DIDN'T EVEN
FAGGOT!
FUCKIN' PSYCHO!
KNOW THIS GUY!
COME HERE! I'M GONNA KILL YOU!
HIS STEEL·BLUE EYES, FRAMED BY STRAW·BLOND HAIR THAT BELONGED ON A CORN FLAKES BOX, EXUDED PURE EVIL. HE WOULD TORMENT ME NON-STOP FOR 3 YEARS.

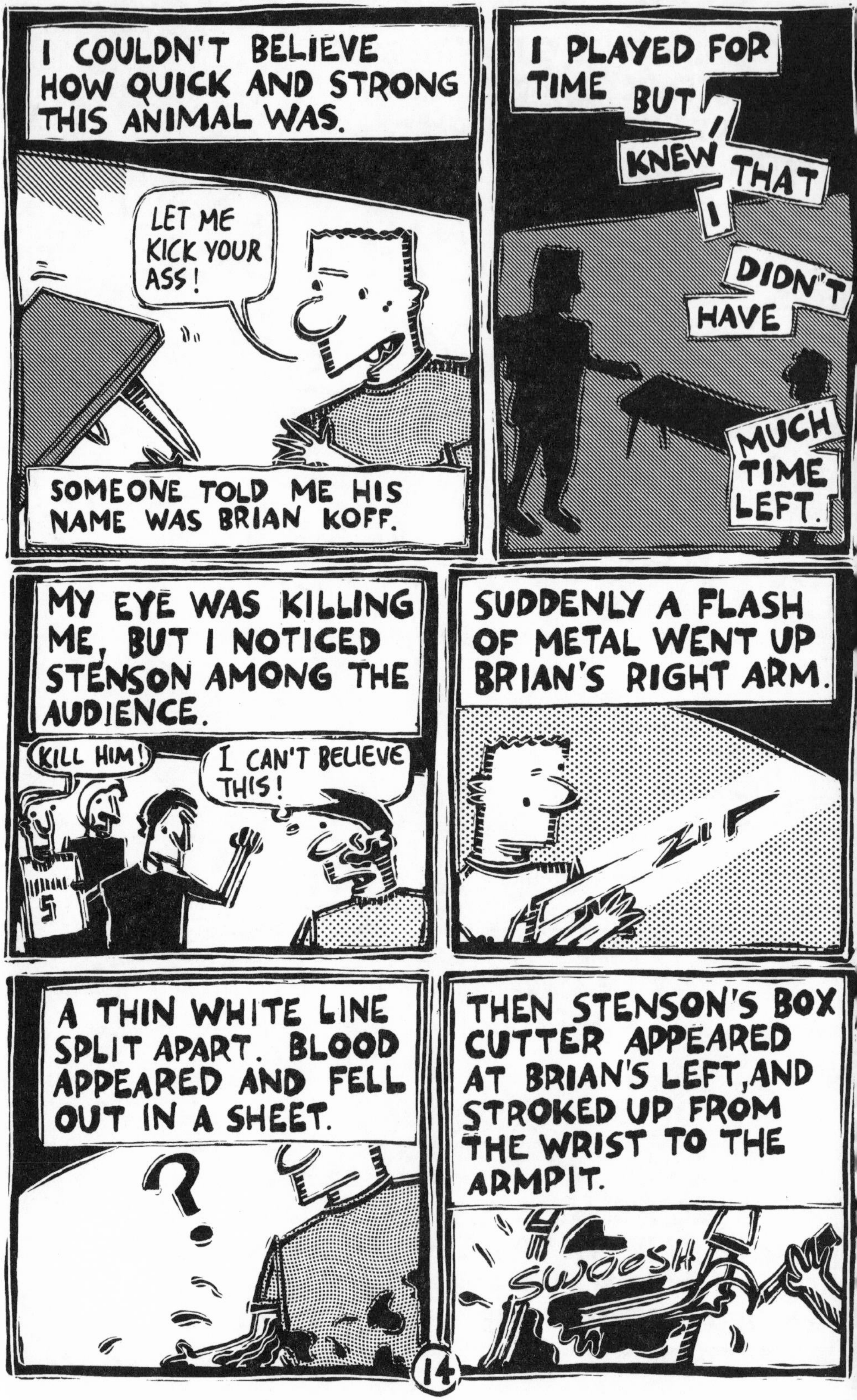
I COULDN'T BELIEVE HOW QUICK AND STRONG THIS ANIMAL WAS.
LET ME KICK YOUR ASS!
SOMEONE TOLD ME HIS NAME WAS BRIAN KOFF.
I PLAYED FOR TIME. BUT I KNEW THAT I DIDN'T HAVE MUCH TIME LEFT.
MY EYE WAS KILLING ME, BUT I NOTICED STENSON AMONG THE AUDIENCE.
KILL HIM!
I CAN'T BELIEVE THIS!
SUDDENLY A FLASH OF METAL WENT UP BRIAN'S RIGHT ARM.
ZIP
A THIN WHITE LINE SPLIT APART. BLOOD APPEARED AND FELL OUT IN A SHEET.
?
THEN STENSON'S BOX CUTTER APPEARED AT BRIAN'S LEFT, AND STROKED UP FROM THE WRIST TO THE ARMPIT.
SWOOSH

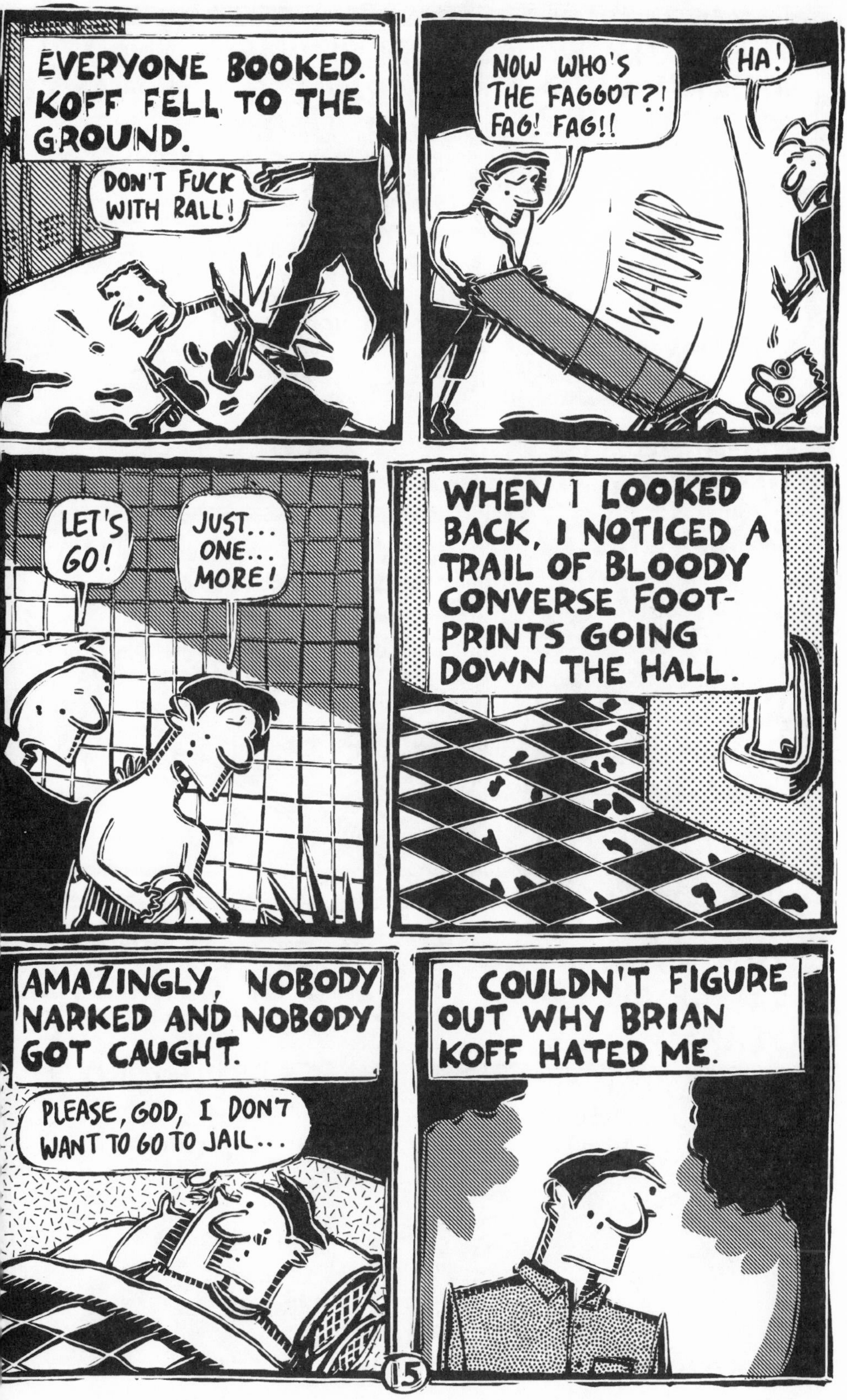
EVERYONE BOOKED. KOFF FELL TO THE GROUND.
DON'T FUCK WITH RALL!
NOW WHO'S THE FAGGOT?! FAG! FAG!!
HA!
WHAM
LET'S GO!
JUST... ONE... MORE!
WHEN I LOOKED BACK, I NOTICED A TRAIL OF BLOODY CONVERSE FOOT-PRINTS GOING DOWN THE HALL.
AMAZINGLY, NOBODY NARKED AND NOBODY GOT CAUGHT.
PLEASE, GOD, I DON'T WANT TO GO TO JAIL...
I COULDN'T FIGURE OUT WHY BRIAN KOFF HATED ME.

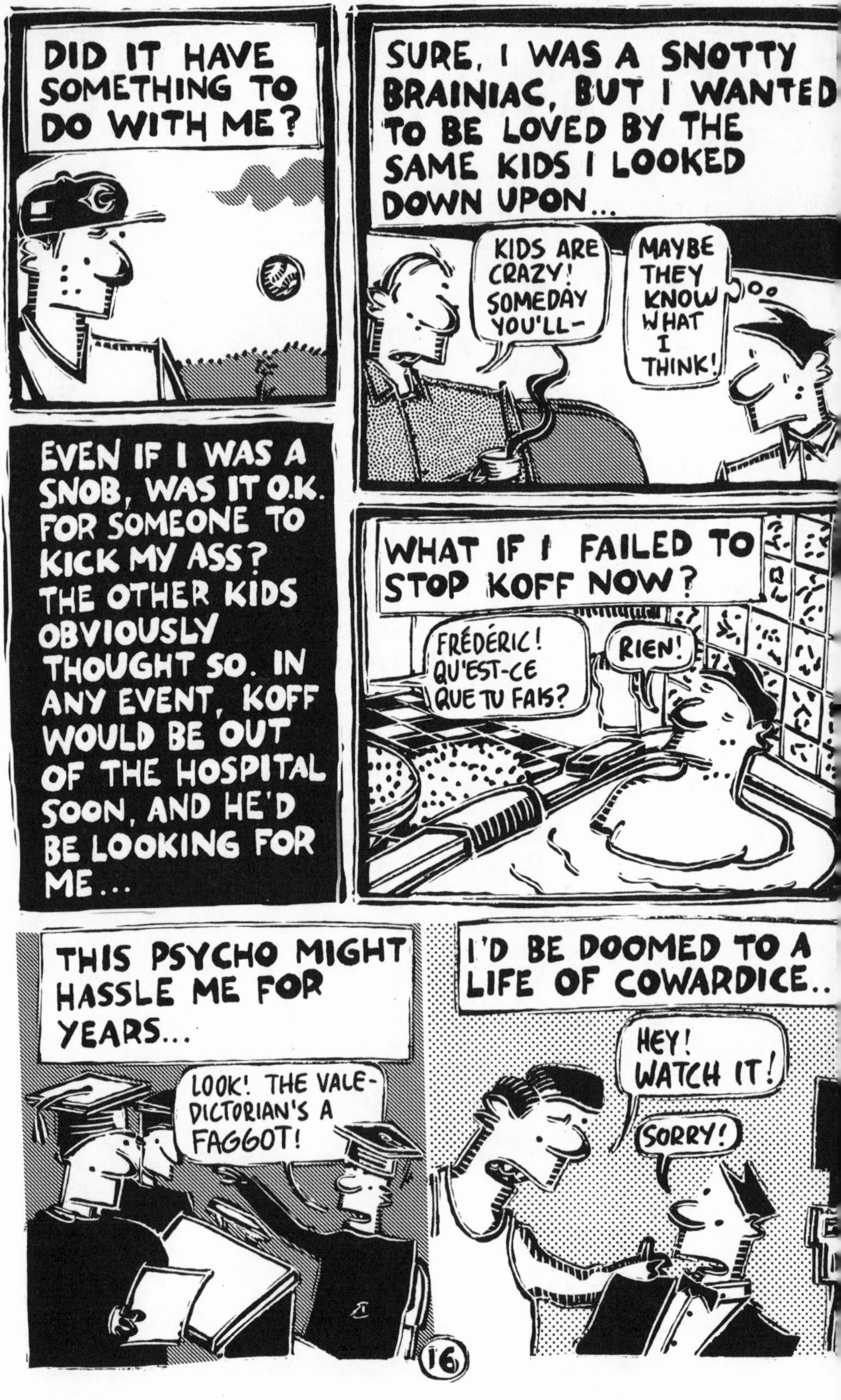
DID IT HAVE SOMETHING TO DO WITH ME?
SURE, I WAS A SNOTTY BRAINIAC, BUT I WANTED TO BE LOVED BY THE SAME KIDS I LOOKED DOWN UPON...
KIDS ARE CRAZY! SOMEDAY YOU'LL-
MAYBE THEY KNOW WHAT I THINK!
EVEN IF I WAS A SNOB, WAS IT O.K. FOR SOMEONE TO KICK MY ASS? THE OTHER KIDS OBVIOUSLY THOUGHT SO. IN ANY EVENT, KOFF WOULD BE OUT OF THE HOSPITAL SOON, AND HE'D BE LOOKING FOR ME...
WHAT IF I FAILED TO STOP KOFF NOW?
FRÉDÉRIC! QU'EST-CE QUE TU FAIS?
RIEN!
THIS PSYCHO MIGHT HASSLE ME FOR YEARS...
LOOK! THE VALE-DICTORIAN'S A FAGGOT!
I'D BE DOOMED TO A LIFE OF COWARDICE...
HEY! WATCH IT!
SORRY!

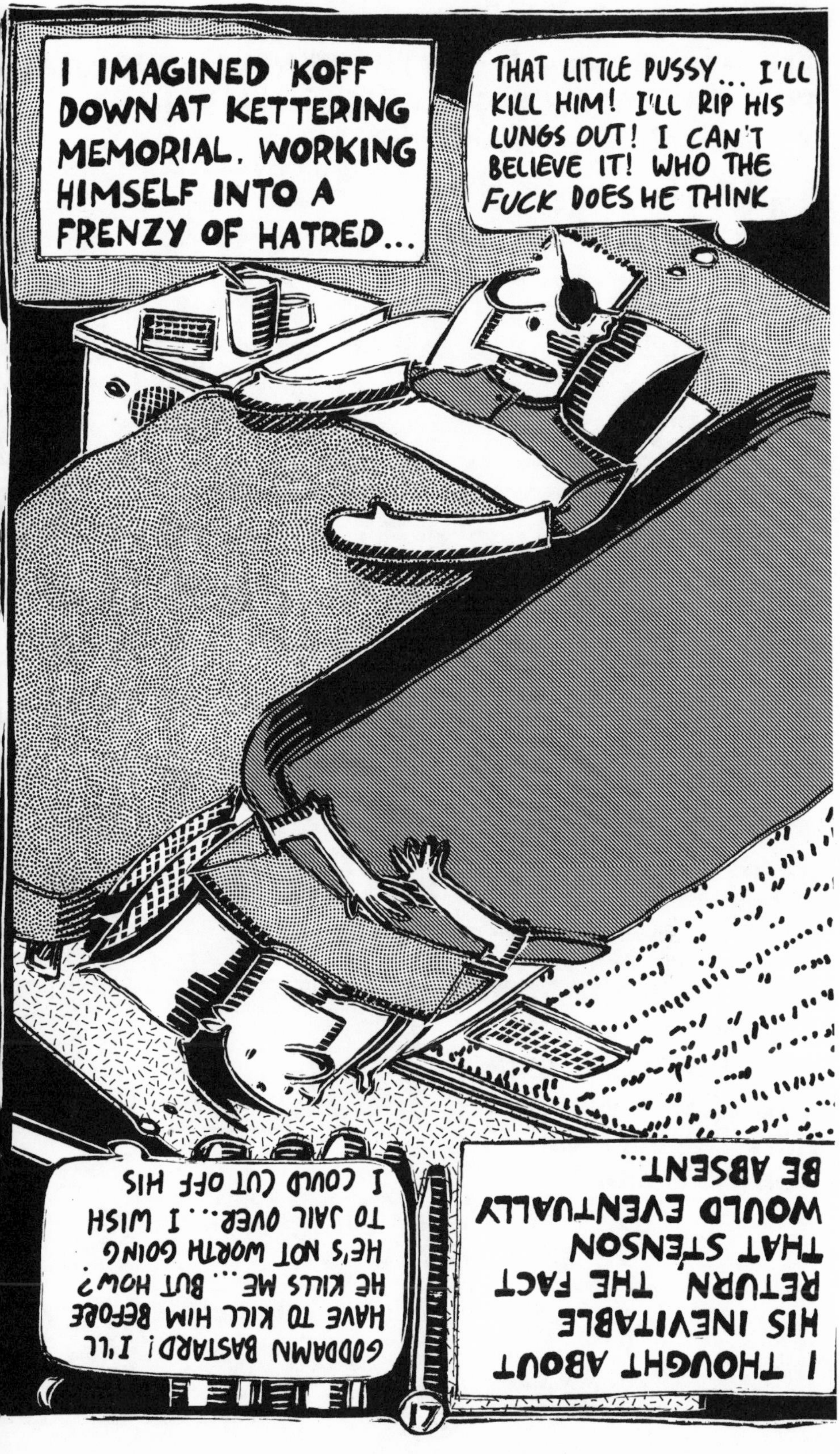
I IMAGINED KOFF DOWN AT KETTERING MEMORIAL. WORKING HIMSELF INTO A FRENZY OF HATRED...
THAT LITTLE PUSSY... I'LL KILL HIM! I'LL RIP HIS LUNGS OUT! I CAN'T BELIEVE IT! WHO THE FUCK DOES HE THINK
I THOUGHT ABOUT HIS INEVITABLE RETURN. THE FACT THAT STENSON WOULD EVENTUALLY BE ABSENT...
GODDAMN BASTARD! I'LL HAVE TO KILL HIM BEFORE HE KILLS ME... BUT HOW? HE'S NOT WORTH GOING TO JAIL OVER... I WISH I COULD CUT OFF HIS

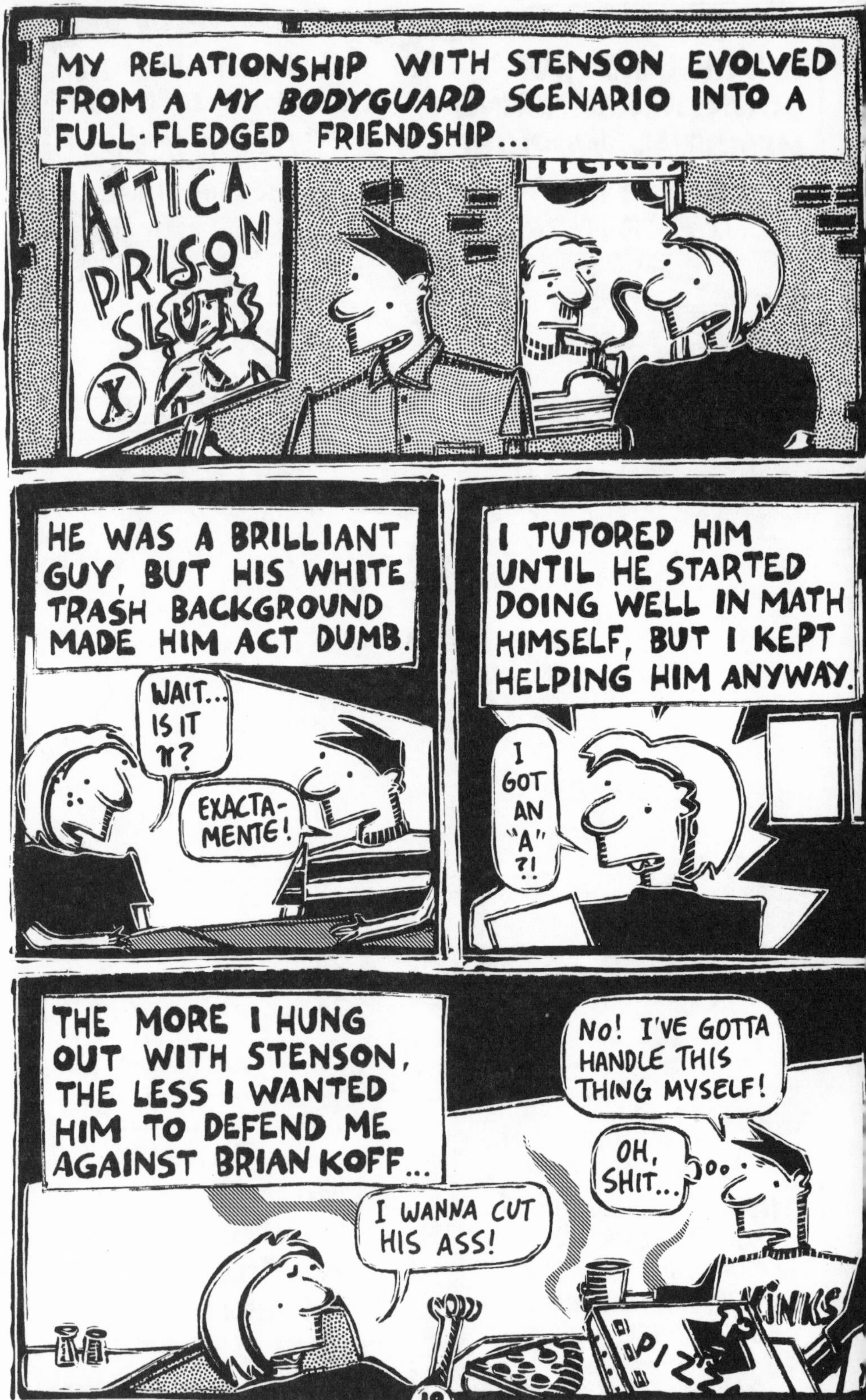
MY RELATIONSHIP WITH STENSON EVOLVED FROM A *MY BODYGUARD* SCENARIO INTO A FULL-FLEDGED FRIENDSHIP...
ATTICA PRISON SLUTS
X
HE WAS A BRILLIANT GUY, BUT HIS WHITE TRASH BACKGROUND MADE HIM ACT DUMB.
WAIT... IS IT π?
EXACTA-MENTE!
I TUTORED HIM UNTIL HE STARTED DOING WELL IN MATH HIMSELF, BUT I KEPT HELPING HIM ANYWAY.
I GOT AN "A" ?!
THE MORE I HUNG OUT WITH STENSON, THE LESS I WANTED HIM TO DEFEND ME AGAINST BRIAN KOFF...
I WANNA CUT HIS ASS!
NO! I'VE GOTTA HANDLE THIS THING MYSELF!
OH, SHIT...
KINKS
PIZ

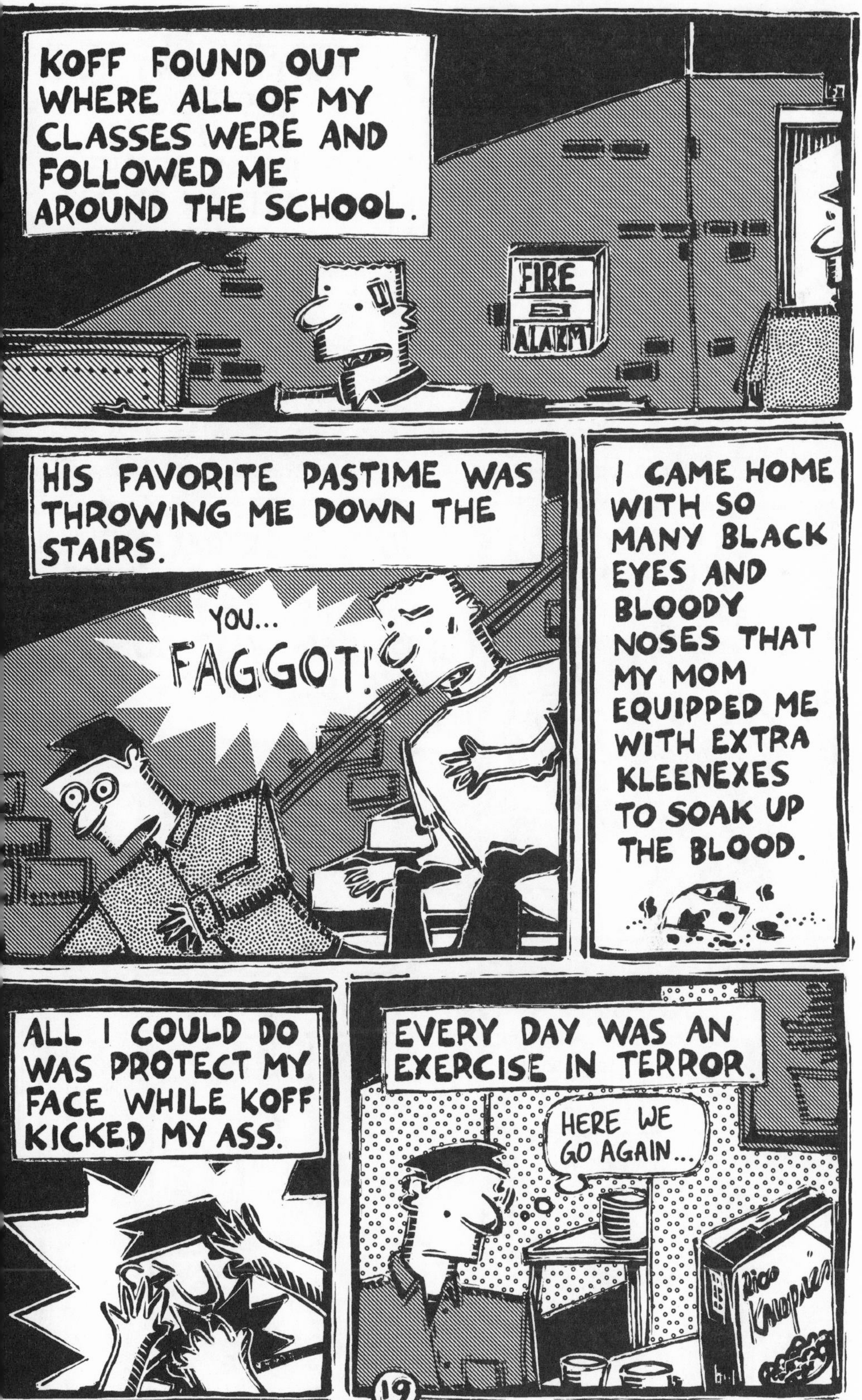
KOFF FOUND OUT WHERE ALL OF MY CLASSES WERE AND FOLLOWED ME AROUND THE SCHOOL.
FIRE ALARM
HIS FAVORITE PASTIME WAS THROWING ME DOWN THE STAIRS.
YOU... FAGGOT!
I CAME HOME WITH SO MANY BLACK EYES AND BLOODY NOSES THAT MY MOM EQUIPPED ME WITH EXTRA KLEENEXES TO SOAK UP THE BLOOD.
ALL I COULD DO WAS PROTECT MY FACE WHILE KOFF KICKED MY ASS.
EVERY DAY WAS AN EXERCISE IN TERROR.
HERE WE GO AGAIN...

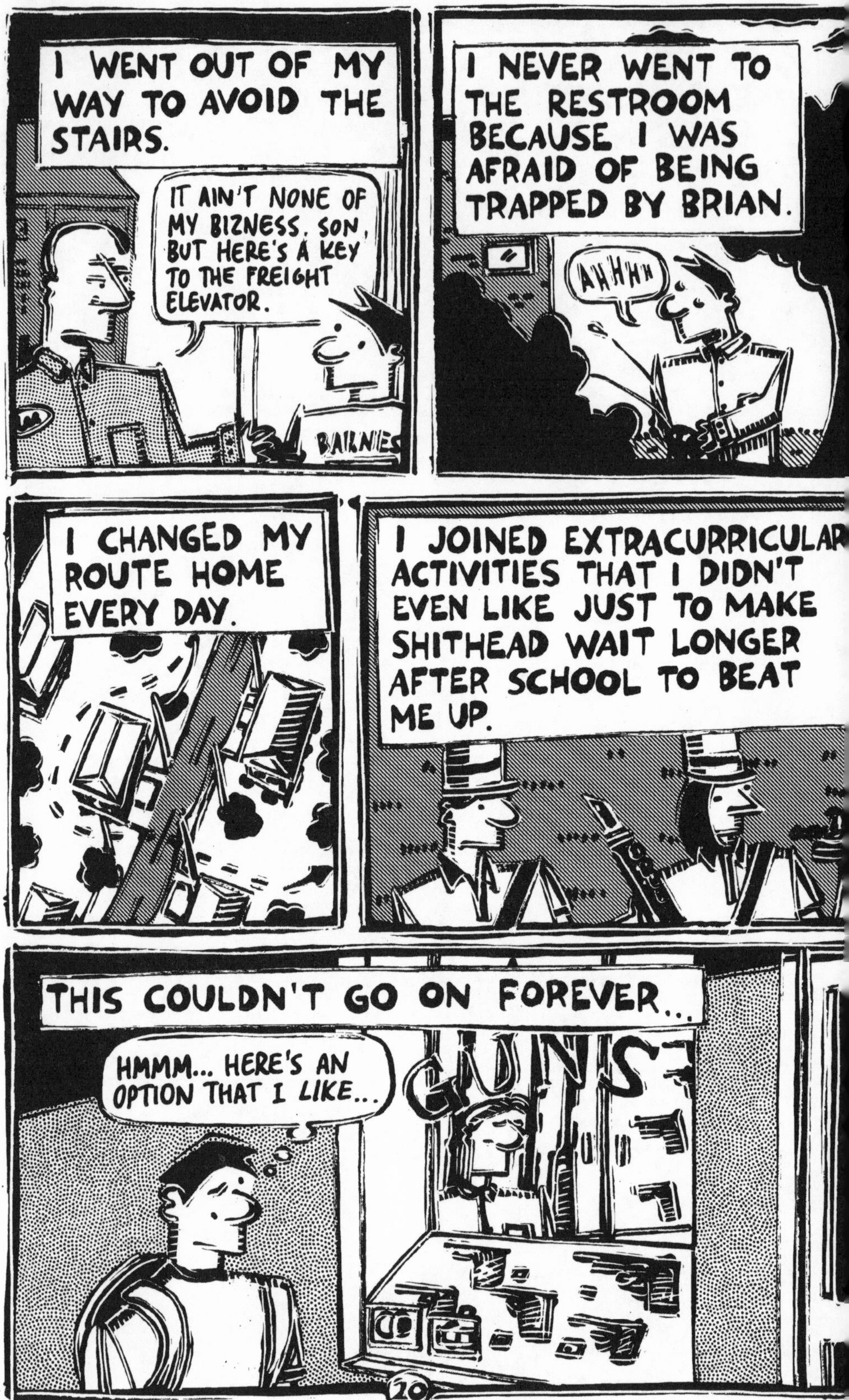
I WENT OUT OF MY WAY TO AVOID THE STAIRS.
IT AIN'T NONE OF MY BIZNESS, SON, BUT HERE'S A KEY TO THE FREIGHT ELEVATOR.
BARNES
I NEVER WENT TO THE RESTROOM BECAUSE I WAS AFRAID OF BEING TRAPPED BY BRIAN.
AHHHH
I CHANGED MY ROUTE HOME EVERY DAY.
I JOINED EXTRACURRICULAR ACTIVITIES THAT I DIDN'T EVEN LIKE JUST TO MAKE SHITHEAD WAIT LONGER AFTER SCHOOL TO BEAT ME UP.
THIS COULDN'T GO ON FOREVER...
HMMM... HERE'S AN OPTION THAT I LIKE...
GUNS

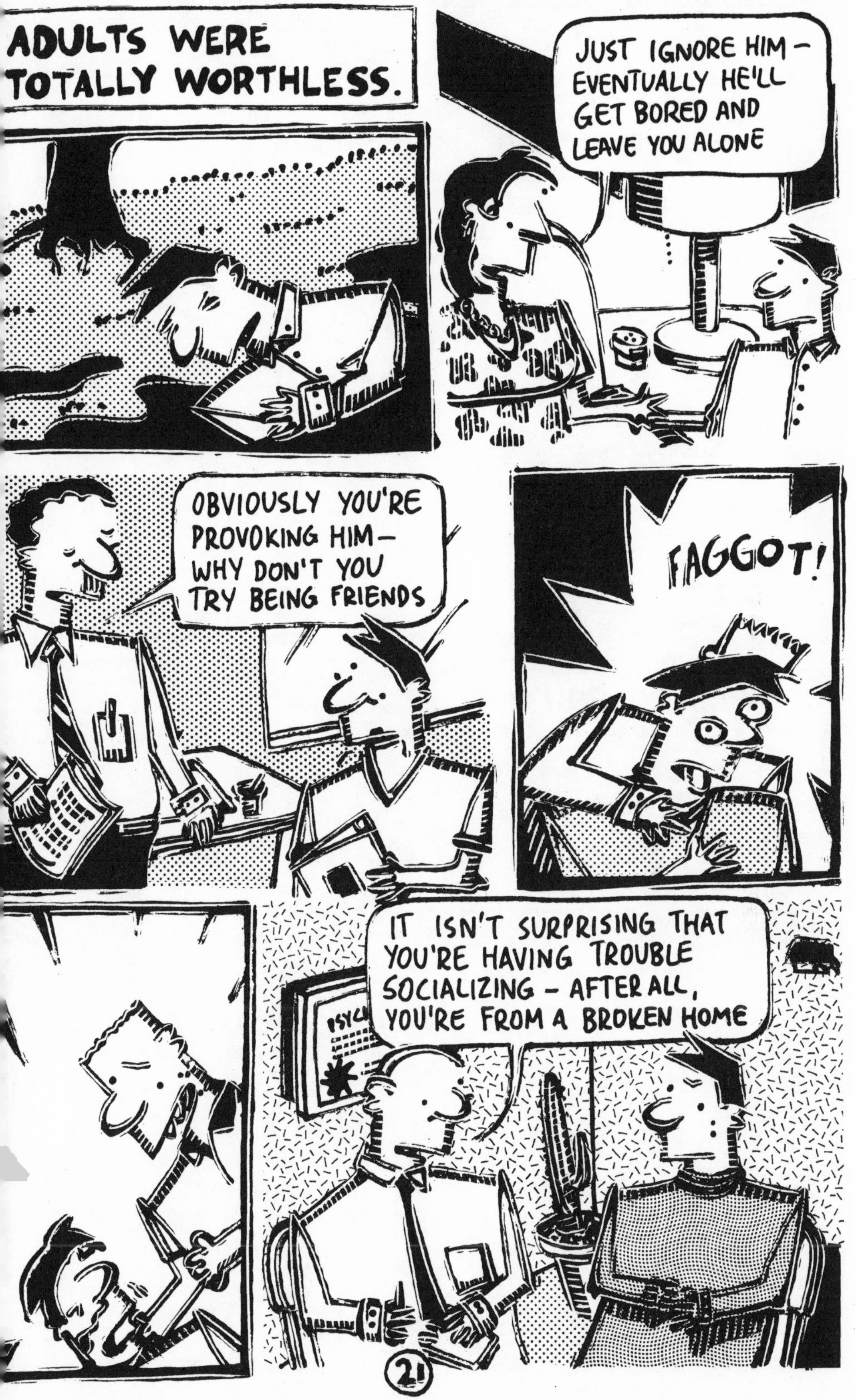
ADULTS WERE TOTALLY WORTHLESS.
JUST IGNORE HIM - EVENTUALLY HE'LL GET BORED AND LEAVE YOU ALONE
OBVIOUSLY YOU'RE PROVOKING HIM - WHY DON'T YOU TRY BEING FRIENDS
FAGGOT!
IT ISN'T SURPRISING THAT YOU'RE HAVING TROUBLE SOCIALIZING - AFTER ALL, YOU'RE FROM A BROKEN HOME

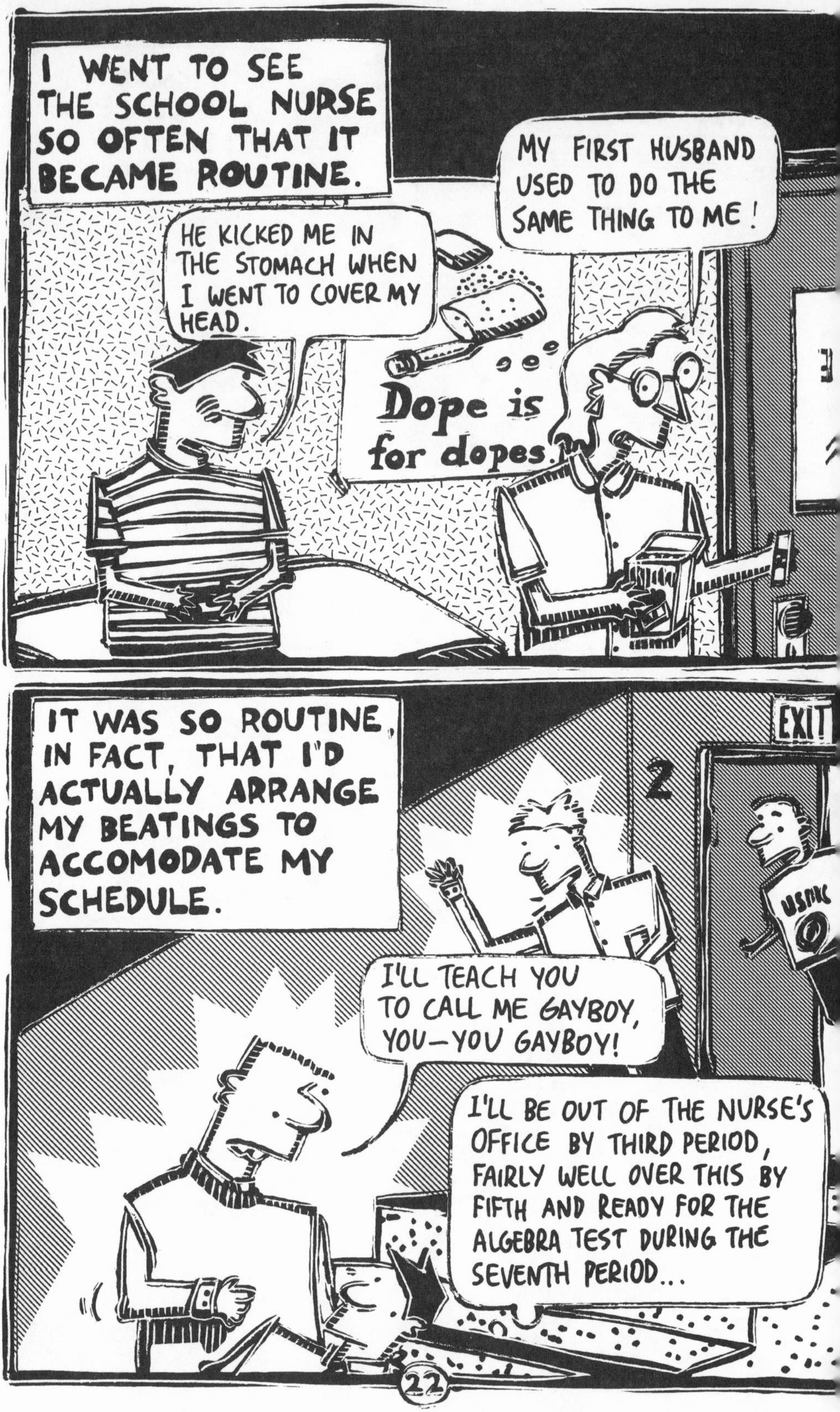
I WENT TO SEE THE SCHOOL NURSE SO OFTEN THAT IT BECAME ROUTINE.
HE KICKED ME IN THE STOMACH WHEN I WENT TO COVER MY HEAD.
MY FIRST HUSBAND USED TO DO THE SAME THING TO ME!
Dope is for dopes.
IT WAS SO ROUTINE, IN FACT, THAT I'D ACTUALLY ARRANGE MY BEATINGS TO ACCOMODATE MY SCHEDULE.
EXIT
2
I'LL TEACH YOU TO CALL ME GAYBOY, YOU—YOU GAYBOY!
I'LL BE OUT OF THE NURSE'S OFFICE BY THIRD PERIOD, FAIRLY WELL OVER THIS BY FIFTH AND READY FOR THE ALGEBRA TEST DURING THE SEVENTH PERIOD...

-4-
SCISSORS, ROCK, HEAD

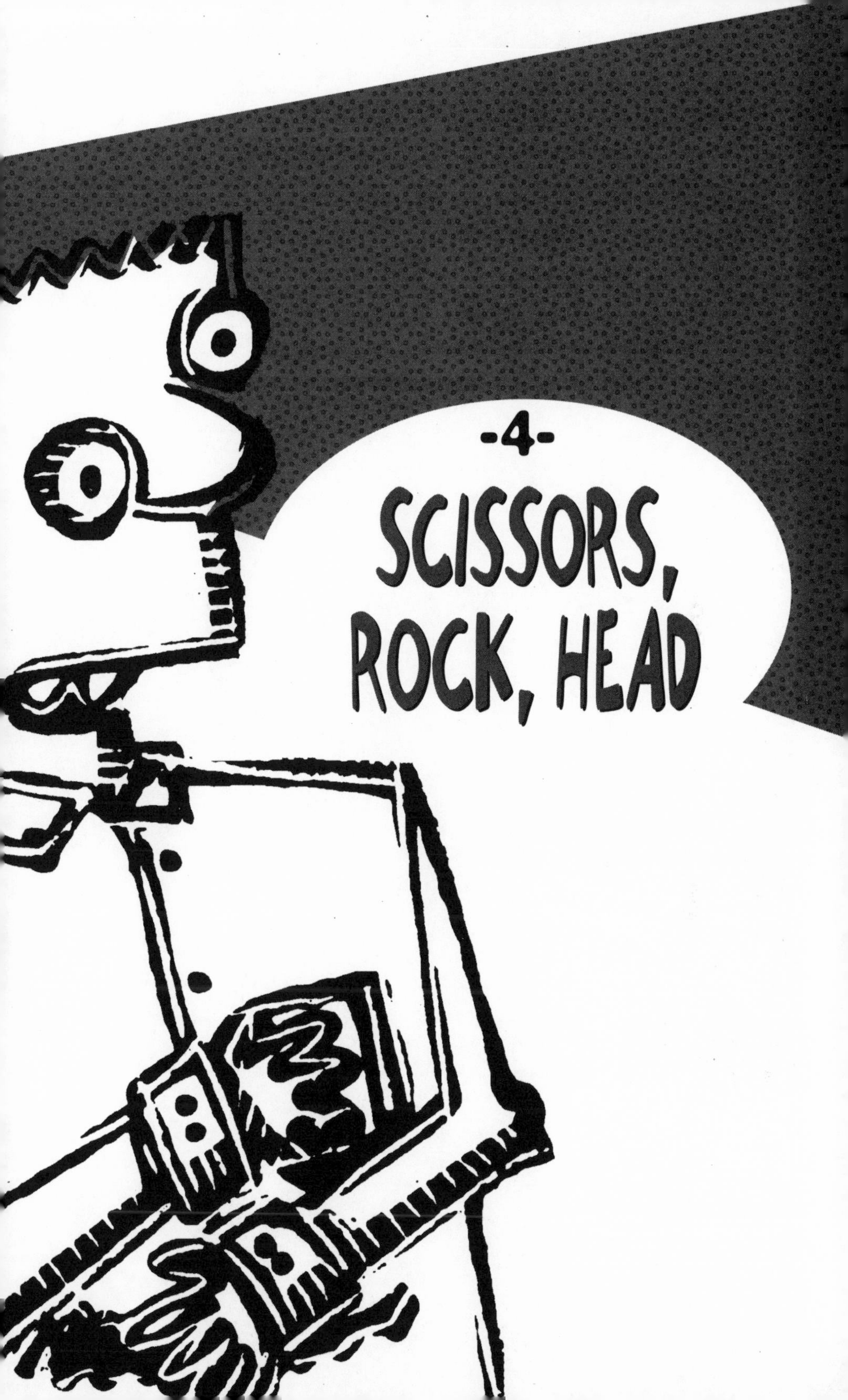

THE THING IS, KOFF WAS MY ONLY PROBLEM. NO ONE ELSE PICKED ON ME, MY GRADES WERE GREAT AND I LIKED MY CLASSES.

HE MADE ME FEEL UNHAPPY TO BE ALIVE. LOGIC DICTATED THAT EVERYTHING WOULD BE GREAT IF HE WASN'T AROUND.

EEEEEEEE! FUCK!

I SAW MY FIRST OPPORTUNITY DURING METAL SHOP CLASS— THE FIRST TIME KOFF WAS IN ONE OF MY CLASSES.

I WAITED FOR KOFF TO SIGN UP FOR THE DRILL PRESS. I MADE SURE TO BE THE FIRST PERSON IN CLASS THE NEXT DAY.

NEXT TO THE DRILL PRESS WAS A BOX OF GNARLED DRILL BITS DEEMED TOO WORN OUT TO BE USED ANYMORE. THEY WERE SOLD FOR SCRAP.

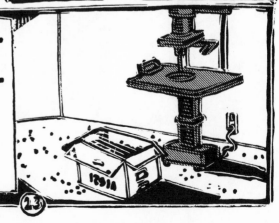

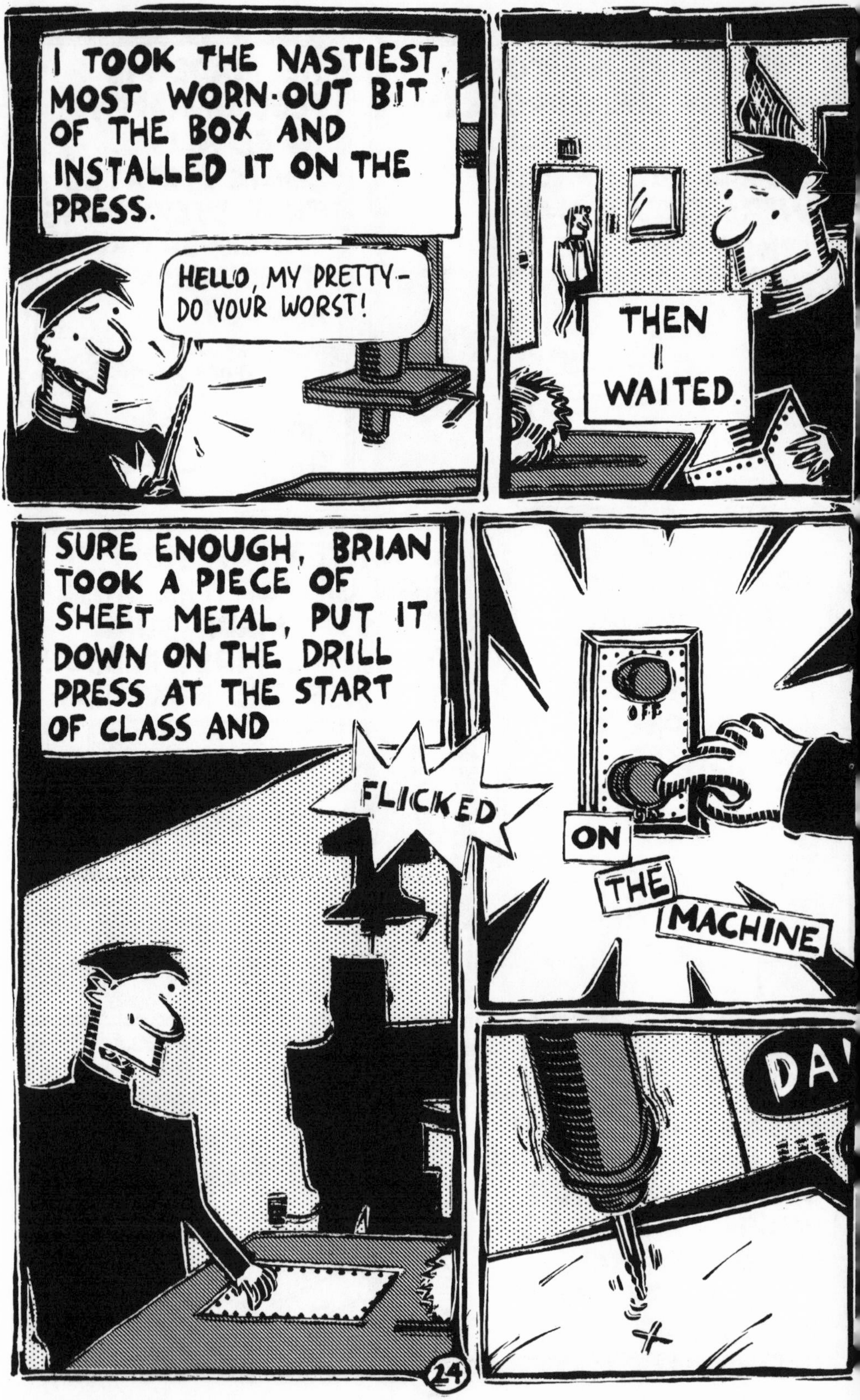

I TOOK THE NASTIEST, MOST WORN-OUT BIT OF THE BOX AND INSTALLED IT ON THE PRESS.
HELLO, MY PRETTY- DO YOUR WORST!
THEN I WAITED.
SURE ENOUGH, BRIAN TOOK A PIECE OF SHEET METAL, PUT IT DOWN ON THE DRILL PRESS AT THE START OF CLASS AND
FLICKED
OFF
ON
THE
MACHINE
DA

I WAS ECSTATIC. HE HADN'T BOTHERED TO HOLD DOWN THE METAL WITH A CLAMP!

THE DRILL CAME DOWN SLOWLY, INEVITABLY.

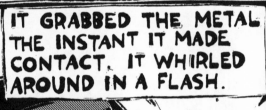

IT GRABBED THE METAL THE INSTANT IT MADE CONTACT. IT WHIRLED AROUND IN A FLASH.

25

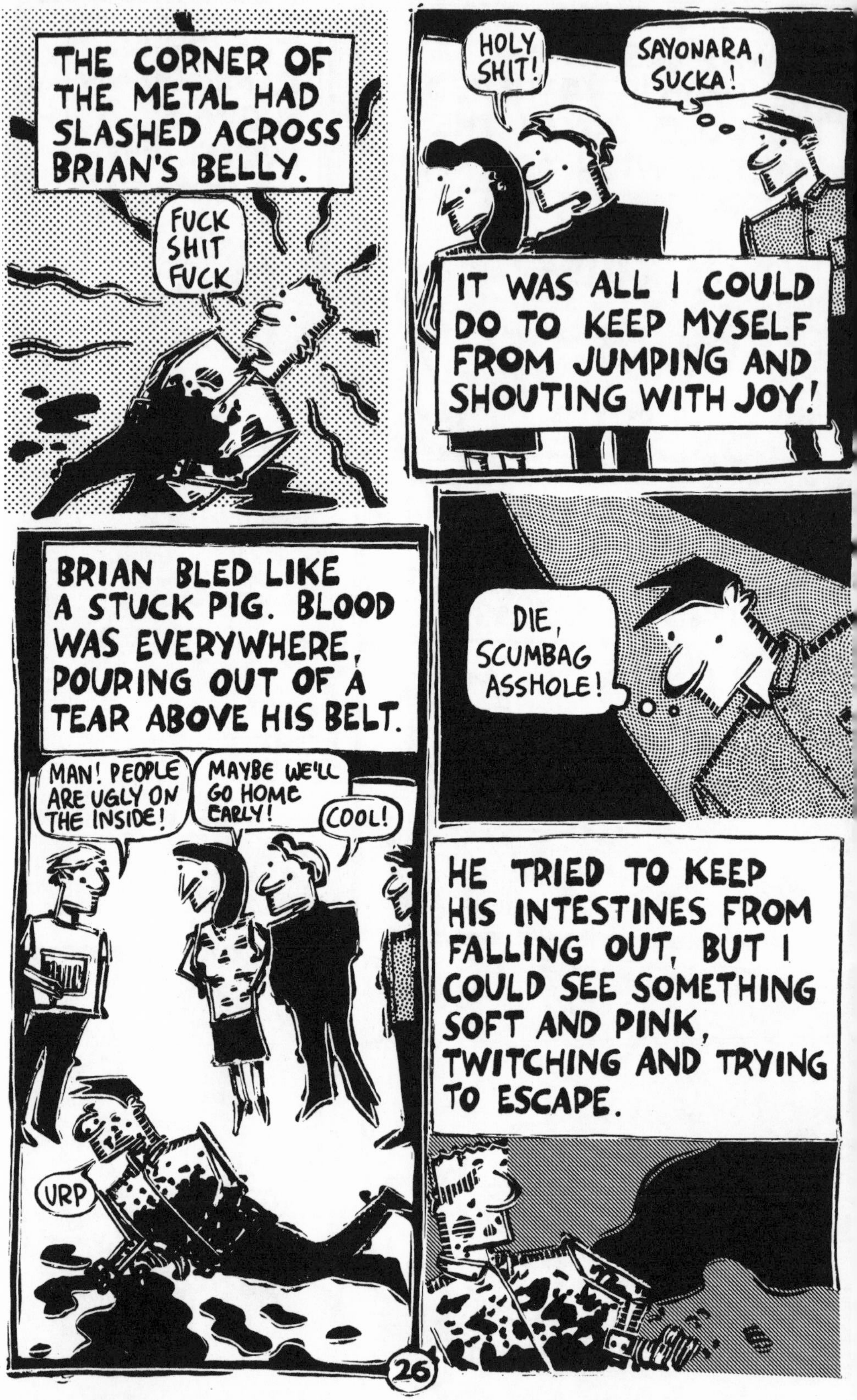
THE CORNER OF THE METAL HAD SLASHED ACROSS BRIAN'S BELLY.
FUCK SHIT FUCK
HOLY SHIT!
SAYONARA, SUCKA!
IT WAS ALL I COULD DO TO KEEP MYSELF FROM JUMPING AND SHOUTING WITH JOY!
BRIAN BLED LIKE A STUCK PIG. BLOOD WAS EVERYWHERE, POURING OUT OF A TEAR ABOVE HIS BELT.
MAN! PEOPLE ARE UGLY ON THE INSIDE!
MAYBE WE'LL GO HOME EARLY!
COOL!
URP
DIE, SCUMBAG ASSHOLE!
HE TRIED TO KEEP HIS INTESTINES FROM FALLING OUT, BUT I COULD SEE SOMETHING SOFT AND PINK, TWITCHING AND TRYING TO ESCAPE.

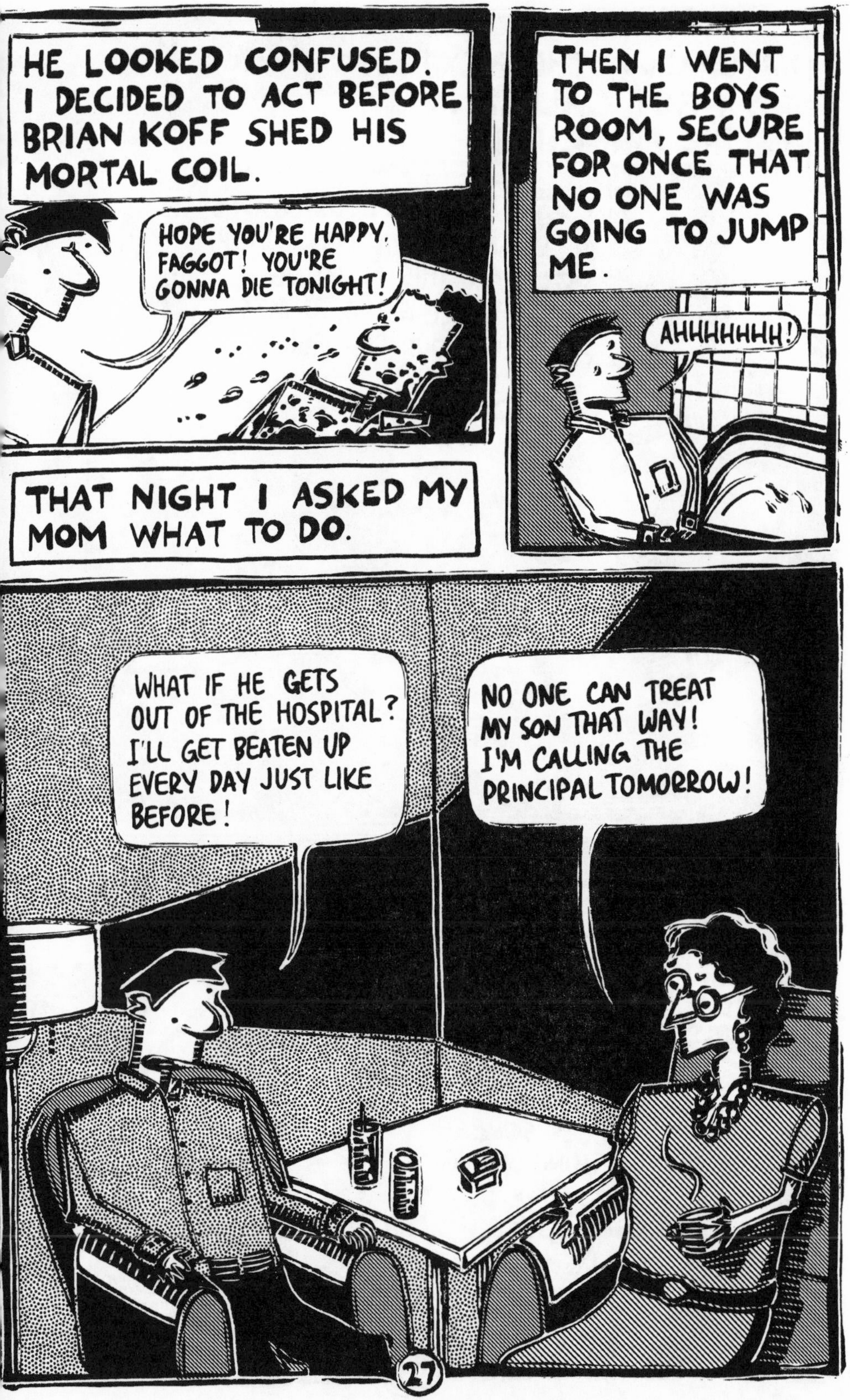
HE LOOKED CONFUSED. I DECIDED TO ACT BEFORE BRIAN KOFF SHED HIS MORTAL COIL.
HOPE YOU'RE HAPPY, FAGGOT! YOU'RE GONNA DIE TONIGHT!
THEN I WENT TO THE BOYS ROOM, SECURE FOR ONCE THAT NO ONE WAS GOING TO JUMP ME.
AHHHHHHH!
THAT NIGHT I ASKED MY MOM WHAT TO DO.
WHAT IF HE GETS OUT OF THE HOSPITAL? I'LL GET BEATEN UP EVERY DAY JUST LIKE BEFORE!
NO ONE CAN TREAT MY SON THAT WAY! I'M CALLING THE PRINCIPAL TOMORROW!

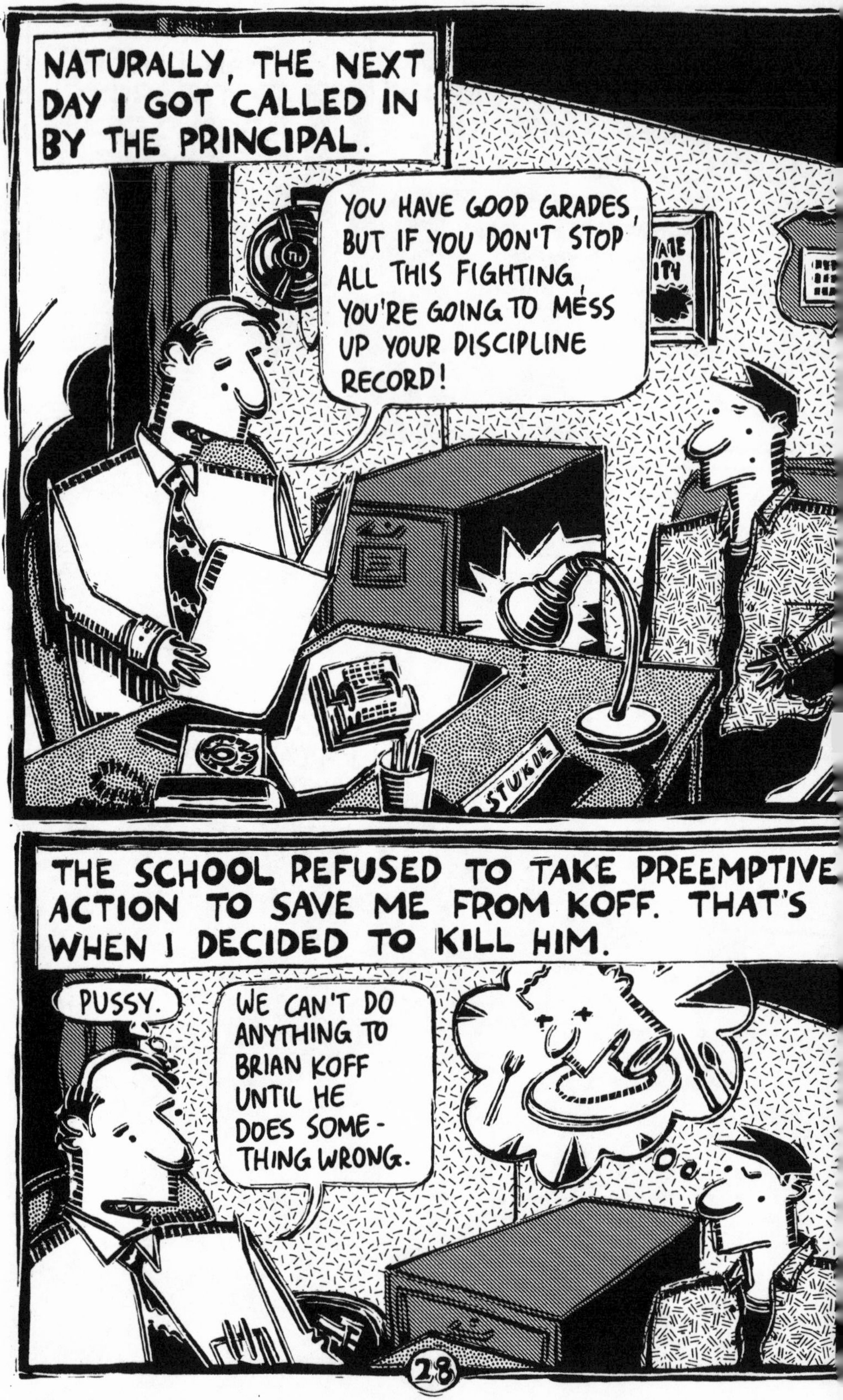
NATURALLY, THE NEXT DAY I GOT CALLED IN BY THE PRINCIPAL.
YOU HAVE GOOD GRADES, BUT IF YOU DON'T STOP ALL THIS FIGHTING, YOU'RE GOING TO MESS UP YOUR DISCIPLINE RECORD!
THE SCHOOL REFUSED TO TAKE PREEMPTIVE ACTION TO SAVE ME FROM KOFF. THAT'S WHEN I DECIDED TO KILL HIM.
PUSSY.
WE CAN'T DO ANYTHING TO BRIAN KOFF UNTIL HE DOES SOME-THING WRONG.

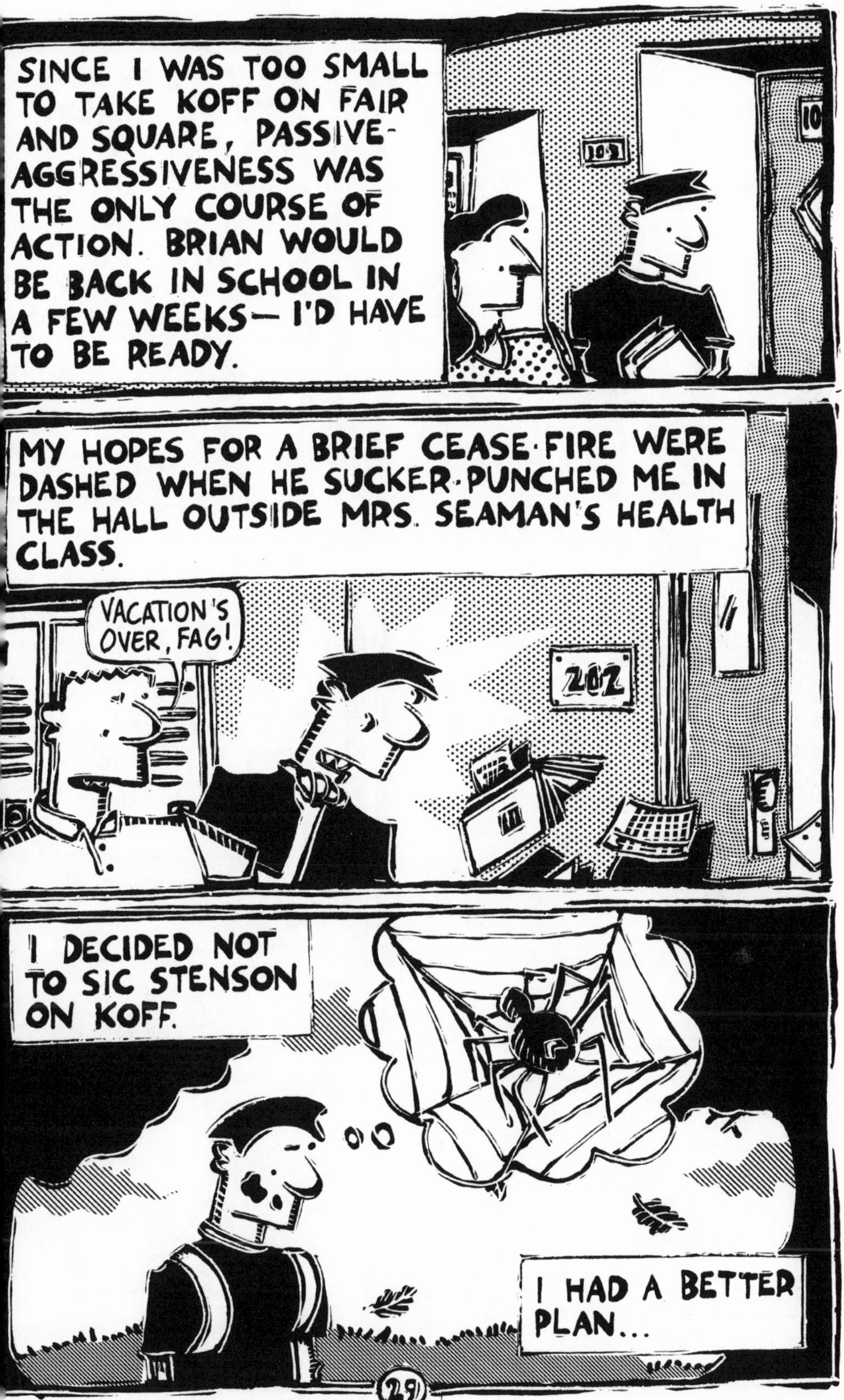

SINCE I WAS TOO SMALL TO TAKE KOFF ON FAIR AND SQUARE, PASSIVE-AGGRESSIVENESS WAS THE ONLY COURSE OF ACTION. BRIAN WOULD BE BACK IN SCHOOL IN A FEW WEEKS— I'D HAVE TO BE READY.
MY HOPES FOR A BRIEF CEASE-FIRE WERE DASHED WHEN HE SUCKER-PUNCHED ME IN THE HALL OUTSIDE MRS. SEAMAN'S HEALTH CLASS.
VACATION'S OVER, FAG!
202
I DECIDED NOT TO SIC STENSON ON KOFF.
I HAD A BETTER PLAN...

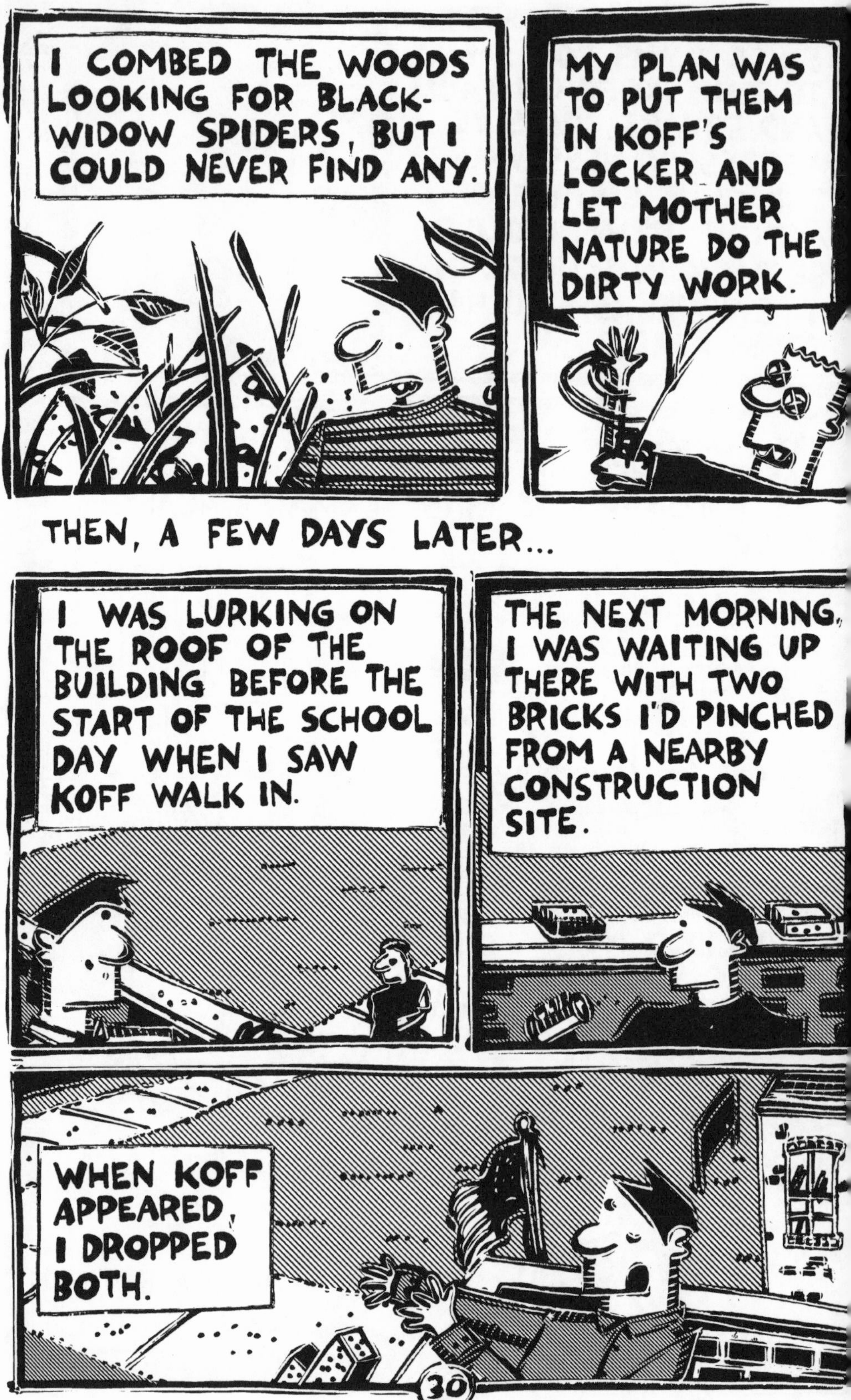
I COMBED THE WOODS LOOKING FOR BLACK-WIDOW SPIDERS, BUT I COULD NEVER FIND ANY.
MY PLAN WAS TO PUT THEM IN KOFF'S LOCKER AND LET MOTHER NATURE DO THE DIRTY WORK.
THEN, A FEW DAYS LATER...
I WAS LURKING ON THE ROOF OF THE BUILDING BEFORE THE START OF THE SCHOOL DAY WHEN I SAW KOFF WALK IN.
THE NEXT MORNING, I WAS WAITING UP THERE WITH TWO BRICKS I'D PINCHED FROM A NEARBY CONSTRUCTION SITE.
WHEN KOFF APPEARED, I DROPPED BOTH.

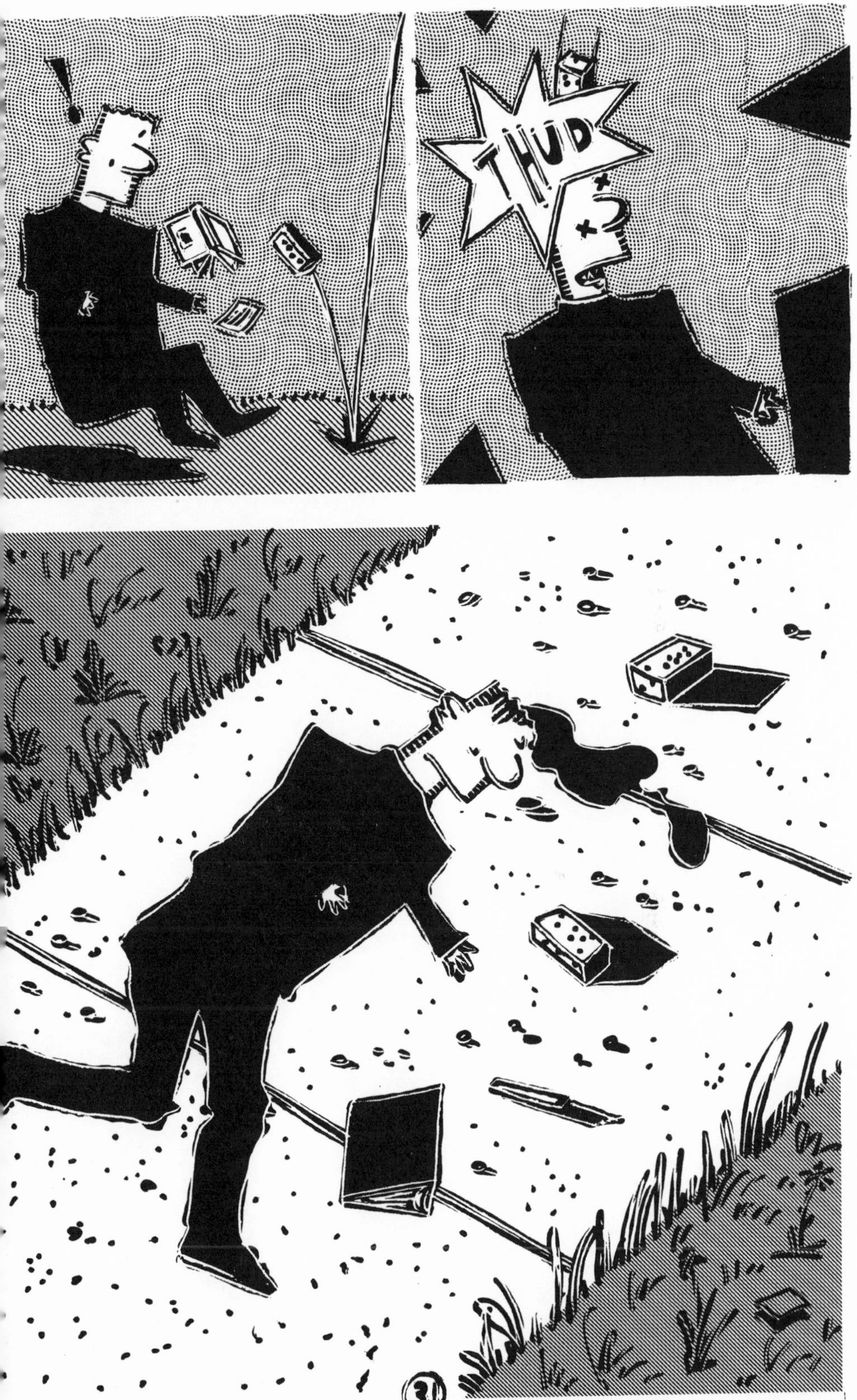
!
THUD

-5-
LIFE IN THE PASSIVE-AGGRESSIVE LANE

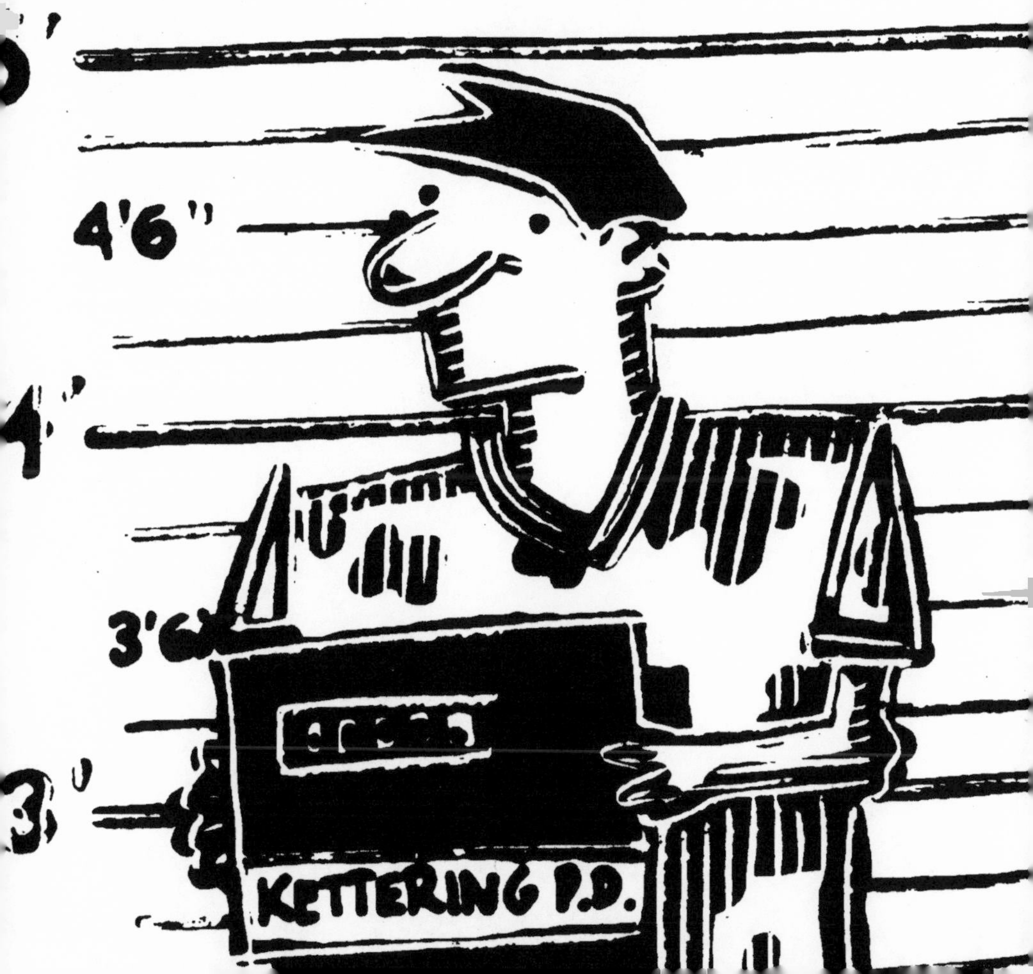

4'6"
3'6"
KETTERING P.D.

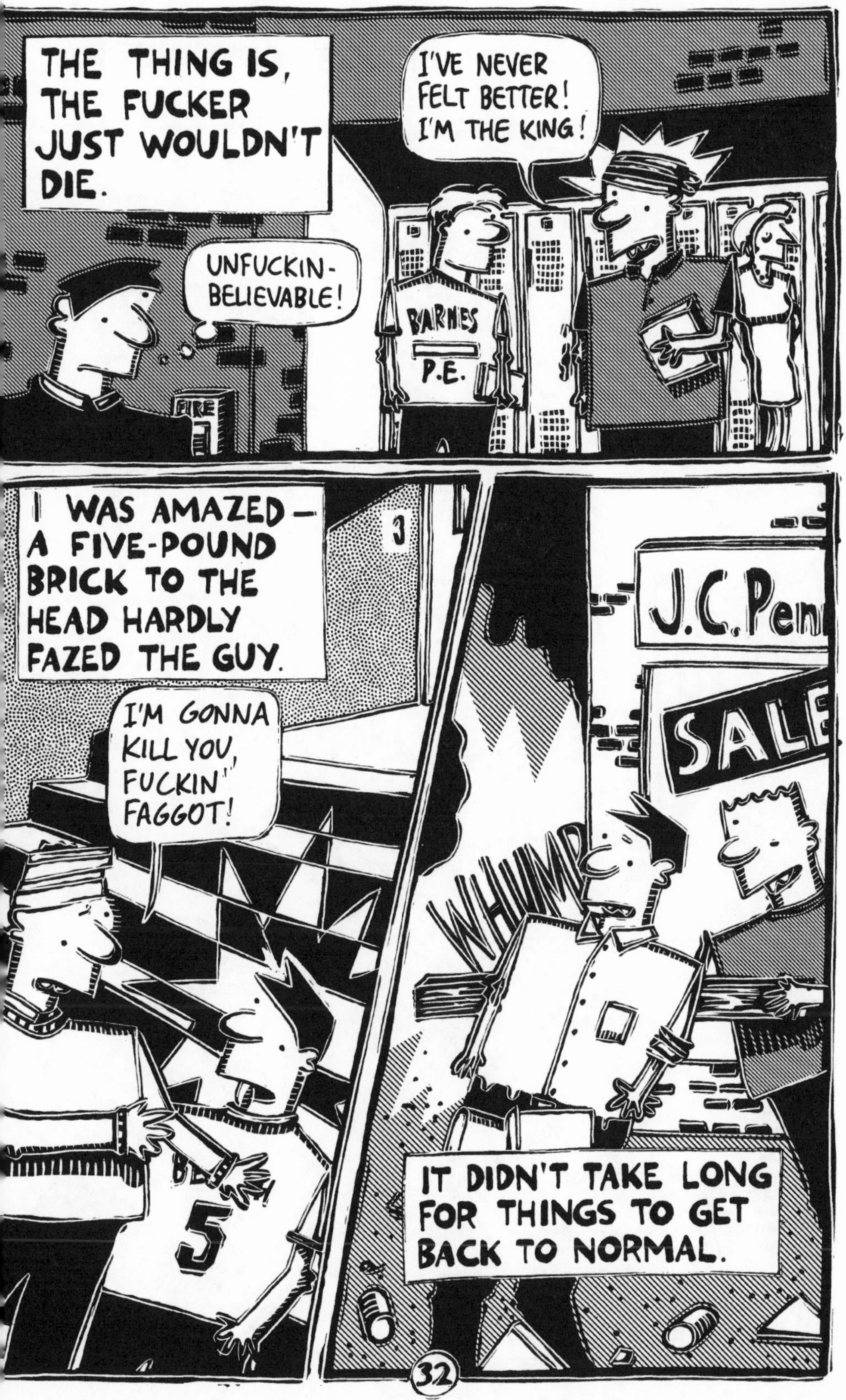
THE THING IS, THE FUCKER JUST WOULDN'T DIE.
I'VE NEVER FELT BETTER! I'M THE KING!
UNFUCKIN-BELIEVABLE!
FIRE
BARNES
P.E.
I WAS AMAZED — A FIVE-POUND BRICK TO THE HEAD HARDLY FAZED THE GUY.
3
I'M GONNA KILL YOU, FUCKIN' FAGGOT!
5
J.C. Pen
SALE
WHUMP
IT DIDN'T TAKE LONG FOR THINGS TO GET BACK TO NORMAL.

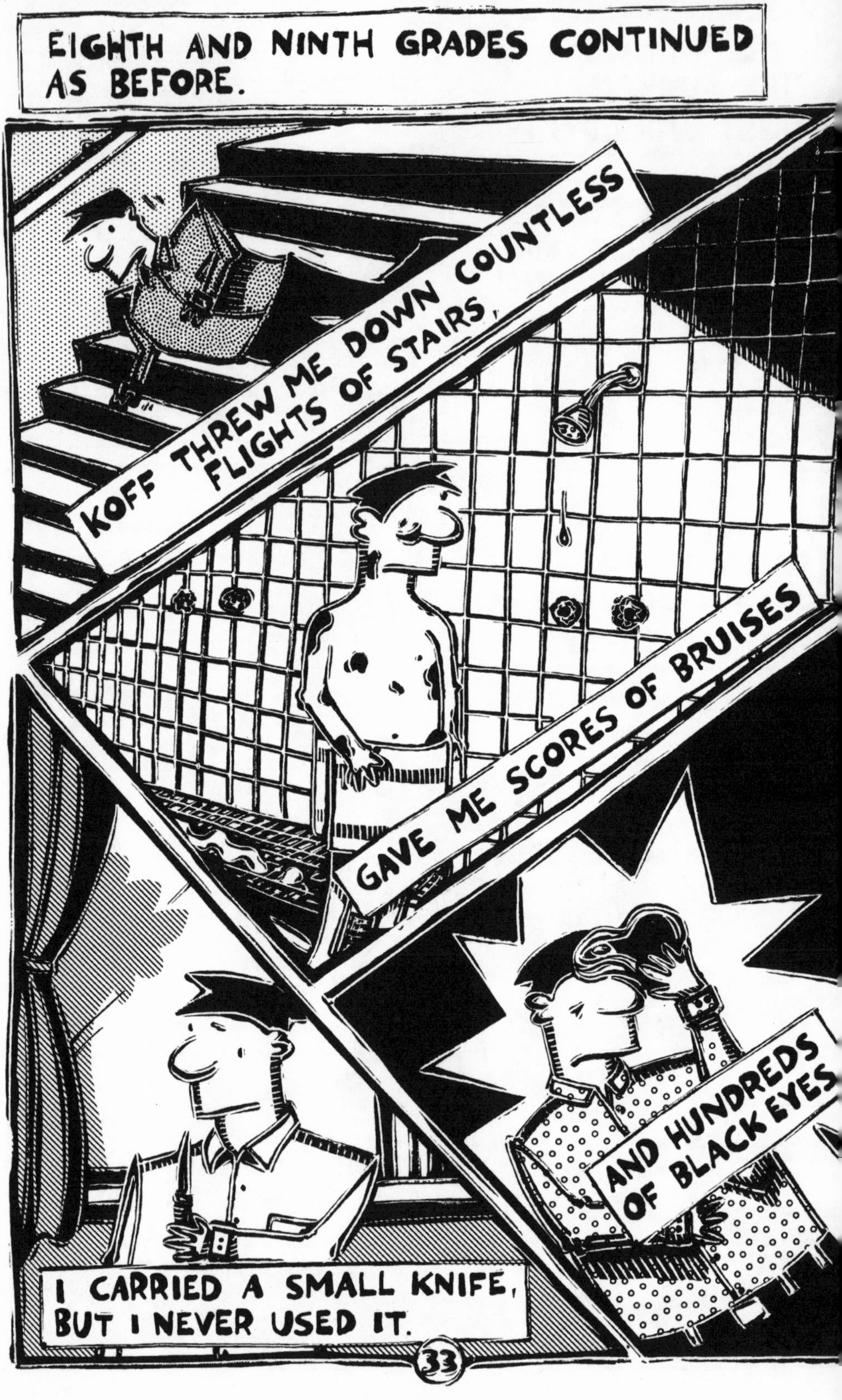
EIGHTH AND NINTH GRADES CONTINUED AS BEFORE.
KOFF THREW ME DOWN COUNTLESS FLIGHTS OF STAIRS,
GAVE ME SCORES OF BRUISES
AND HUNDREDS OF BLACK EYES
I CARRIED A SMALL KNIFE, BUT I NEVER USED IT.

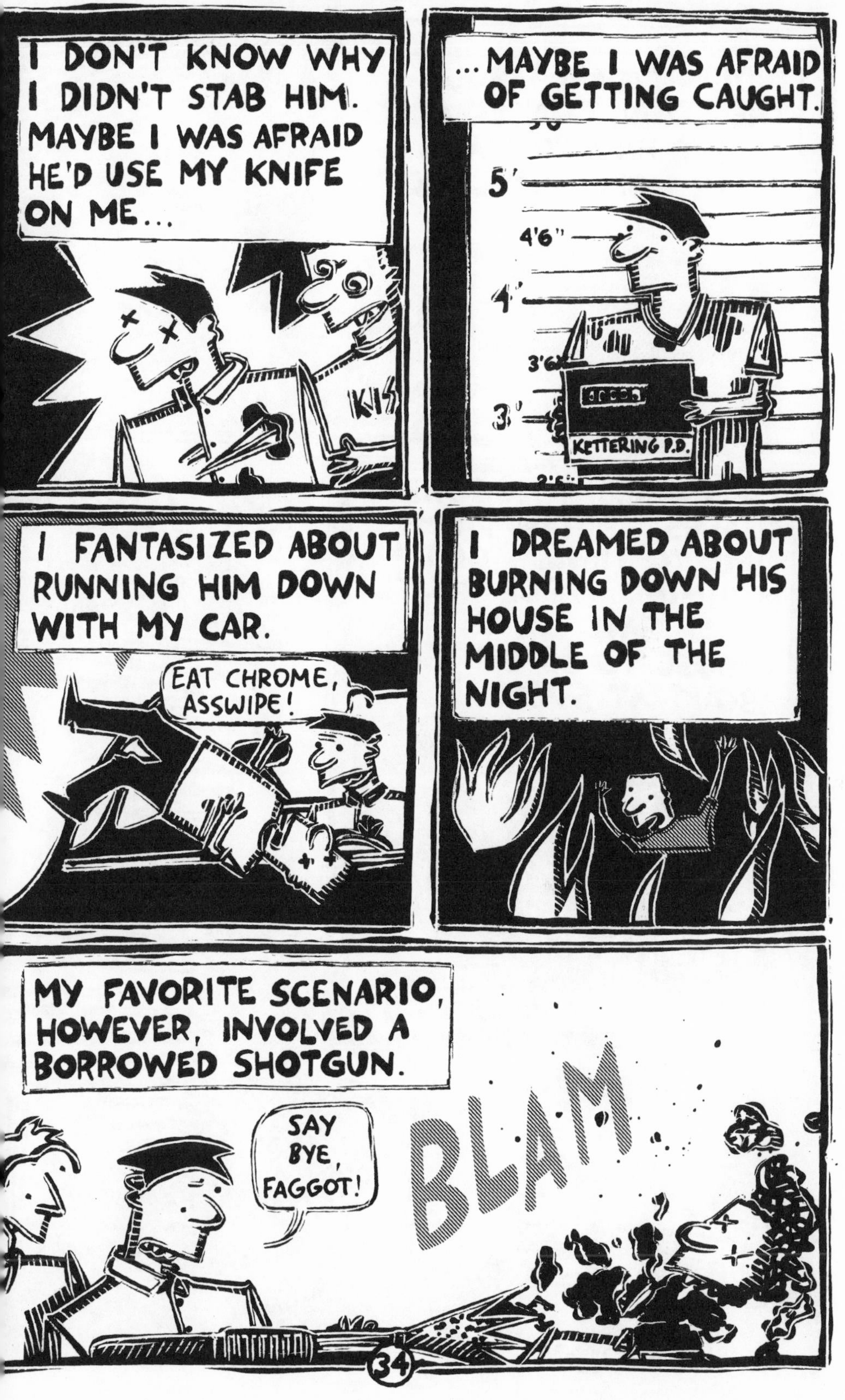
I DON'T KNOW WHY I DIDN'T STAB HIM. MAYBE I WAS AFRAID HE'D USE MY KNIFE ON ME...
...MAYBE I WAS AFRAID OF GETTING CAUGHT.
5'
4'6"
4'
3'6"
3'
KETTERING P.D.
I FANTASIZED ABOUT RUNNING HIM DOWN WITH MY CAR.
EAT CHROME, ASSWIPE!
I DREAMED ABOUT BURNING DOWN HIS HOUSE IN THE MIDDLE OF THE NIGHT.
MY FAVORITE SCENARIO, HOWEVER, INVOLVED A BORROWED SHOTGUN.
SAY BYE, FAGGOT!
BLAM

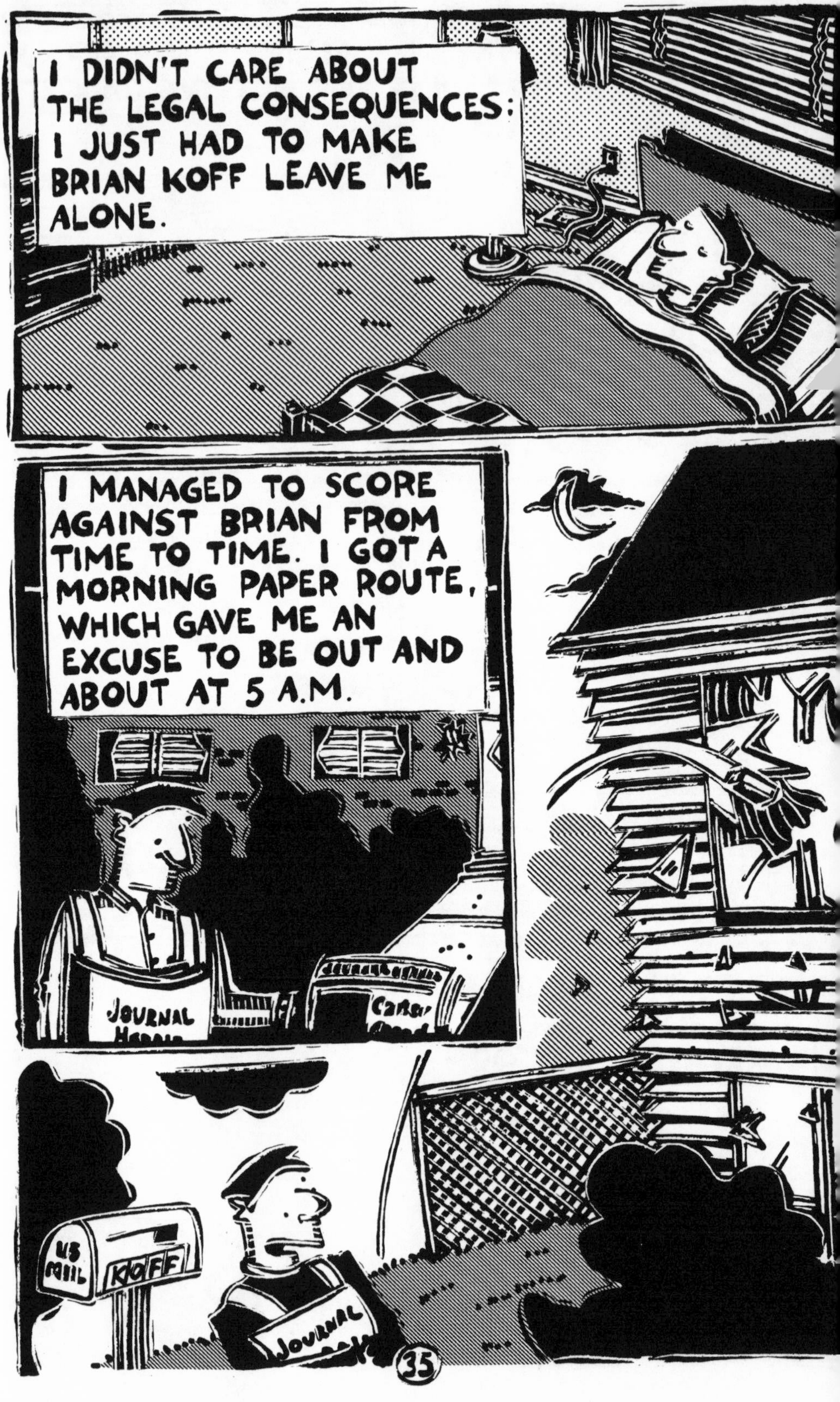
I DIDN'T CARE ABOUT THE LEGAL CONSEQUENCES: I JUST HAD TO MAKE BRIAN KOFF LEAVE ME ALONE.
I MANAGED TO SCORE AGAINST BRIAN FROM TIME TO TIME. I GOT A MORNING PAPER ROUTE, WHICH GAVE ME AN EXCUSE TO BE OUT AND ABOUT AT 5 A.M.
JOURNAL
US MAIL
KOFF
JOURNAL

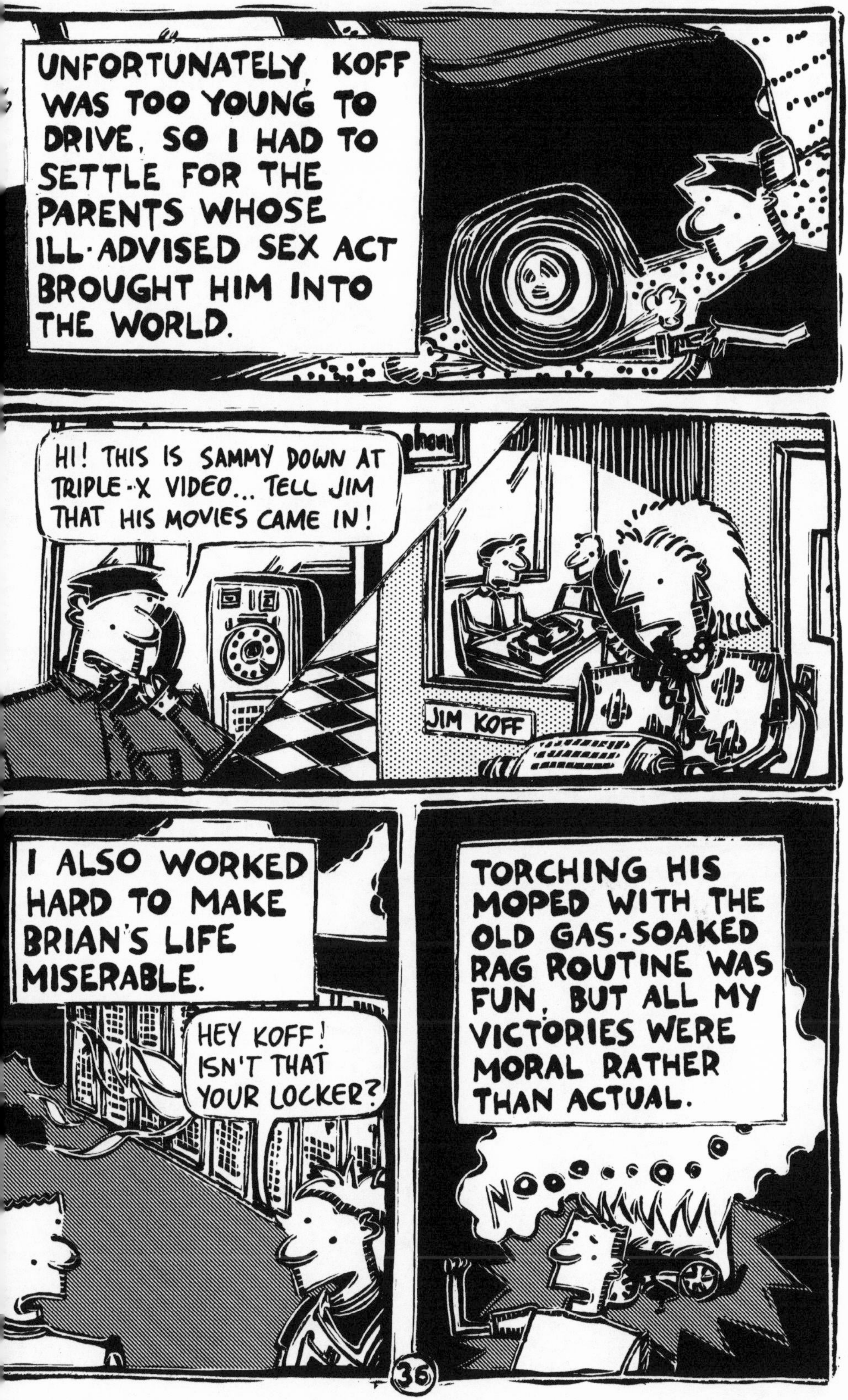
UNFORTUNATELY, KOFF WAS TOO YOUNG TO DRIVE, SO I HAD TO SETTLE FOR THE PARENTS WHOSE ILL-ADVISED SEX ACT BROUGHT HIM INTO THE WORLD.
HI! THIS IS SAMMY DOWN AT TRIPLE-X VIDEO... TELL JIM THAT HIS MOVIES CAME IN!
JIM KOFF
I ALSO WORKED HARD TO MAKE BRIAN'S LIFE MISERABLE.
HEY KOFF! ISN'T THAT YOUR LOCKER?
TORCHING HIS MOPED WITH THE OLD GAS-SOAKED RAG ROUTINE WAS FUN, BUT ALL MY VICTORIES WERE MORAL RATHER THAN ACTUAL.
NOOO...OOO

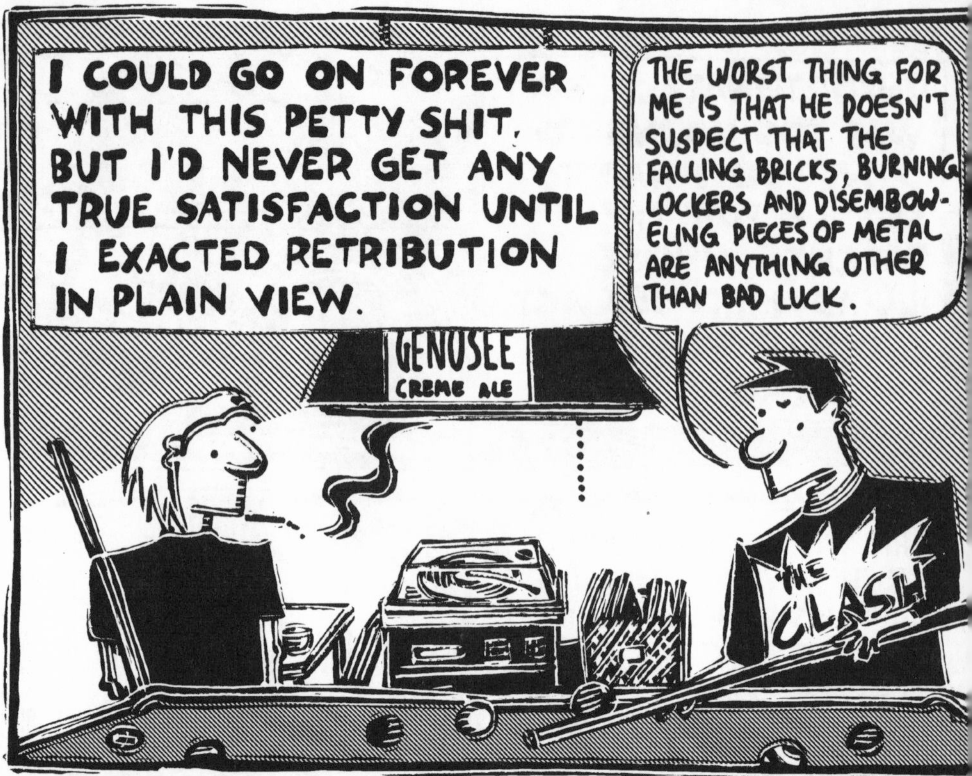
I COULD GO ON FOREVER WITH THIS PETTY SHIT, BUT I'D NEVER GET ANY TRUE SATISFACTION UNTIL I EXACTED RETRIBUTION IN PLAIN VIEW.
THE WORST THING FOR ME IS THAT HE DOESN'T SUSPECT THAT THE FALLING BRICKS, BURNING LOCKERS AND DISEMBOW-ELING PIECES OF METAL ARE ANYTHING OTHER THAN BAD LUCK.
GENUSEE
CREME ALE
THE CLASH

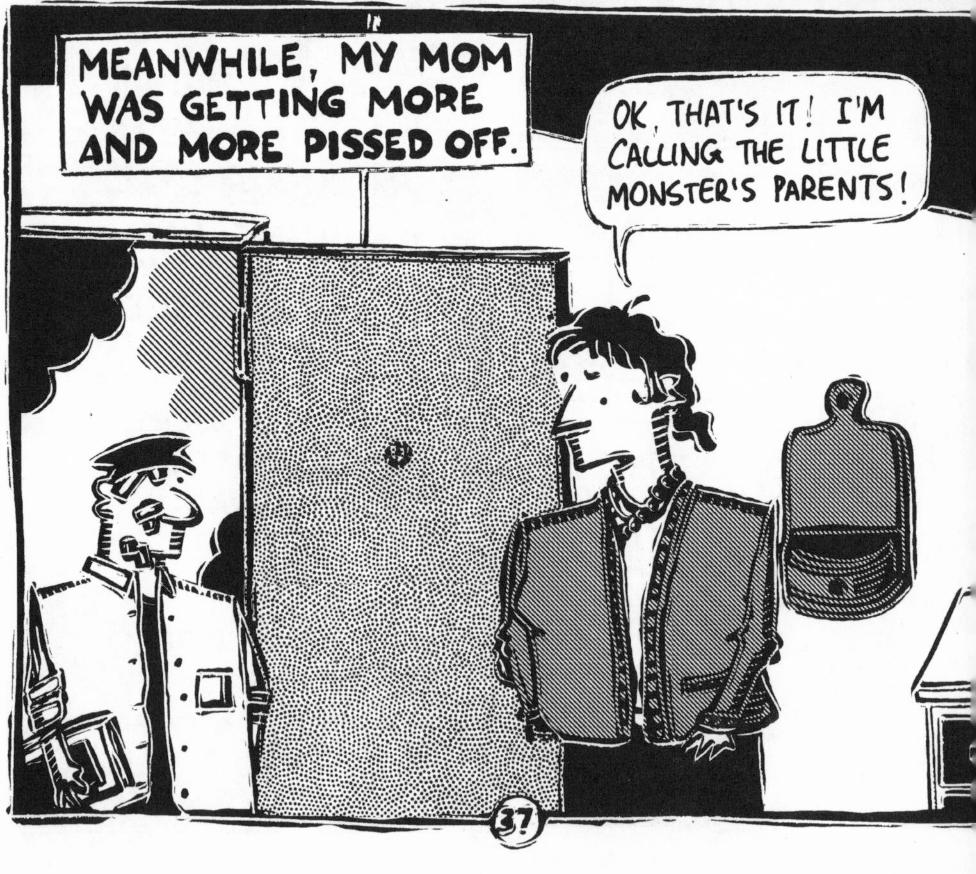
MEANWHILE, MY MOM WAS GETTING MORE AND MORE PISSED OFF.
OK, THAT'S IT! I'M CALLING THE LITTLE MONSTER'S PARENTS!

MOM DID HER BEST, BUT IT DIDN'T DO ANY GOOD.

KIDS HAVE TO WORK THESE THINGS OUT!

EASY FOR YOU TO SAY— YOUR SON ISN'T GETTING HIT EVERY DAY!

TRUE... BECAUSE I DIDN'T RAISE HIM TO BE A BABY!

YOU'RE RIGHT— YOU MADE HIM A BULLY INSTEAD!

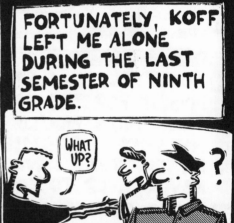

FORTUNATELY, KOFF LEFT ME ALONE DURING THE LAST SEMESTER OF NINTH GRADE.

WHAT UP?

?

EVERYONE WAS EXCITED ABOUT LEAVING FOR HIGH SCHOOL.

I'M GONNA MAJOR IN HOME-EC... IT'LL BE SO EASY THAT I'LL GRADUATE WITH A 4.0 IN 4 YEARS!

GOOD PLAN!

I CONVINCED MYSELF THAT BRIAN HAD CHANGED TOO.

POETRY IS REALLY COOL!

B

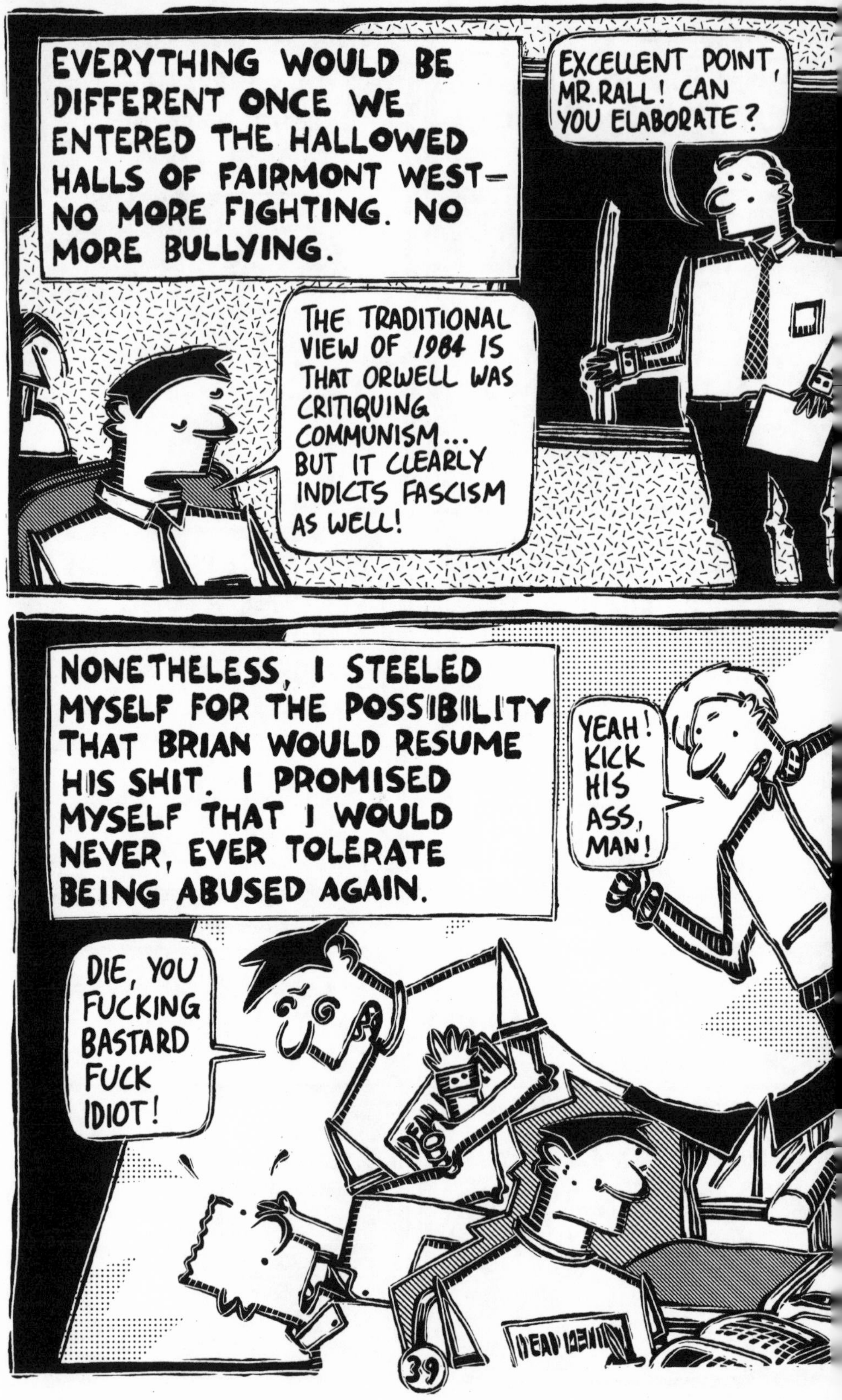
EVERYTHING WOULD BE DIFFERENT ONCE WE ENTERED THE HALLOWED HALLS OF FAIRMONT WEST— NO MORE FIGHTING. NO MORE BULLYING.
EXCELLENT POINT, MR. RALL! CAN YOU ELABORATE?
THE TRADITIONAL VIEW OF 1984 IS THAT ORWELL WAS CRITIQUING COMMUNISM... BUT IT CLEARLY INDICTS FASCISM AS WELL!
NONETHELESS, I STEELED MYSELF FOR THE POSSIBILITY THAT BRIAN WOULD RESUME HIS SHIT. I PROMISED MYSELF THAT I WOULD NEVER, EVER TOLERATE BEING ABUSED AGAIN.
YEAH! KICK HIS ASS, MAN!
DIE, YOU FUCKING BASTARD FUCK IDIOT!

-6-
FINAL EXAM: D-DAY

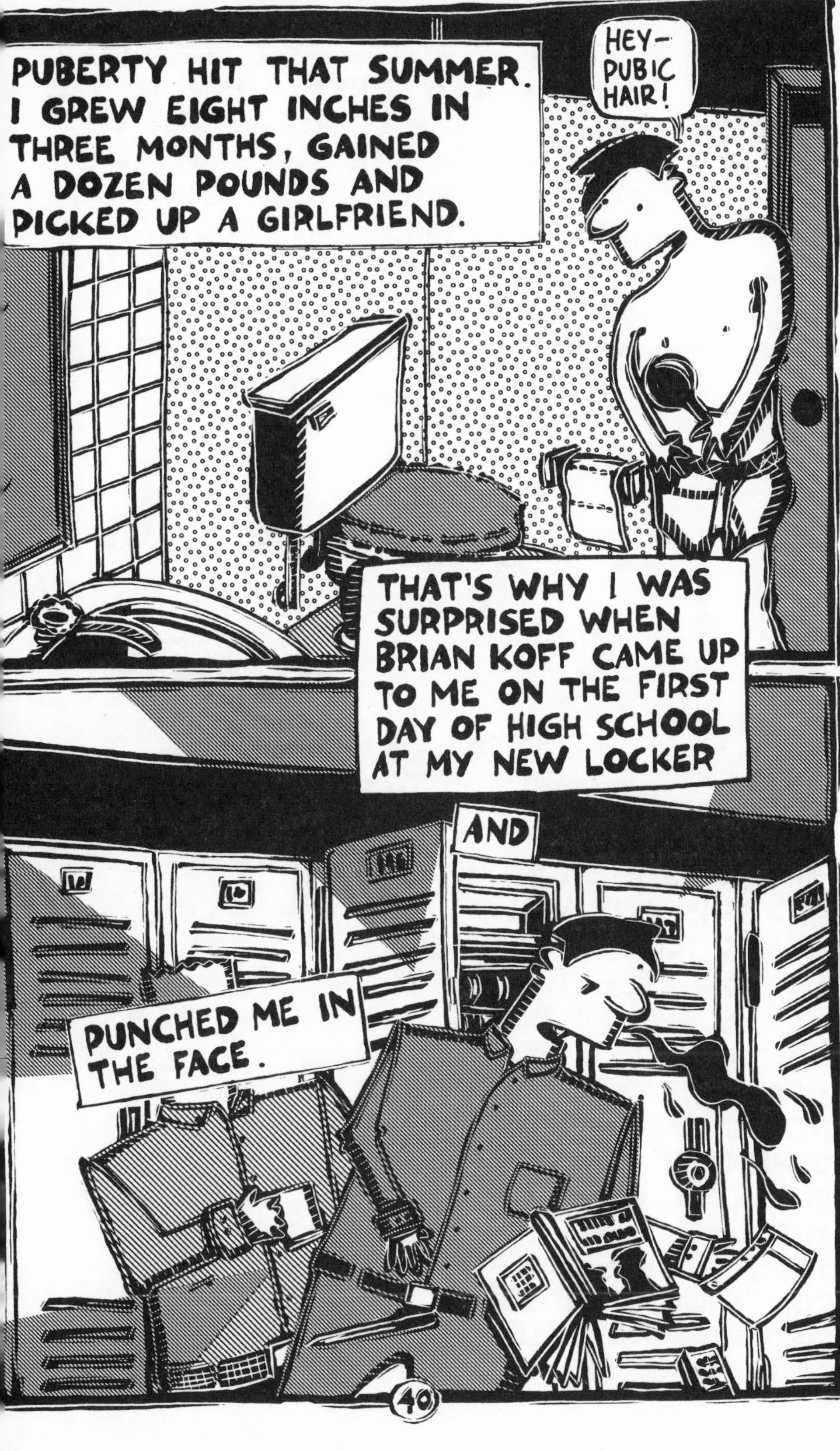

PUBERTY HIT THAT SUMMER. I GREW EIGHT INCHES IN THREE MONTHS, GAINED A DOZEN POUNDS AND PICKED UP A GIRLFRIEND.
HEY- PUBIC HAIR!
THAT'S WHY I WAS SURPRISED WHEN BRIAN KOFF CAME UP TO ME ON THE FIRST DAY OF HIGH SCHOOL AT MY NEW LOCKER
AND
PUNCHED ME IN THE FACE.

I LOOKED DOWN AT KOFF — FOR THE FIRST TIME, I WAS LOOKING *DOWN* — AND AT THAT MOMENT, EVERY OUNCE OF ACCUMULATED HATRED, EVERY BLACK EYE AND BRUISED KNEE, EVERY TIME I'D IMAGINED POUNDING IN HIS SMIRKY ALL-AMERICAN FACE, EVERY TIME I HAD TO HOLD MY PISS OUT OF FEAR... IT ALL CAME BACK.

THIS WAS HIGH SCHOOL, AND THIS SHIT WASN'T GOING TO START HERE. I'D DONE MY THREE YEARS, AND I'D BEEN WILLING TO LET KOFF OFF THE HOOK FOR WHAT HE'D DONE DURING THAT PERIOD OF PRE-HISTORY. BUT KOFF WASN'T ON THE SAME PAGE. HE THOUGHT HIS FUN WOULD CONTINUE UNABATED FOREVER AND EVER AND EVER AND EVER.

(41)

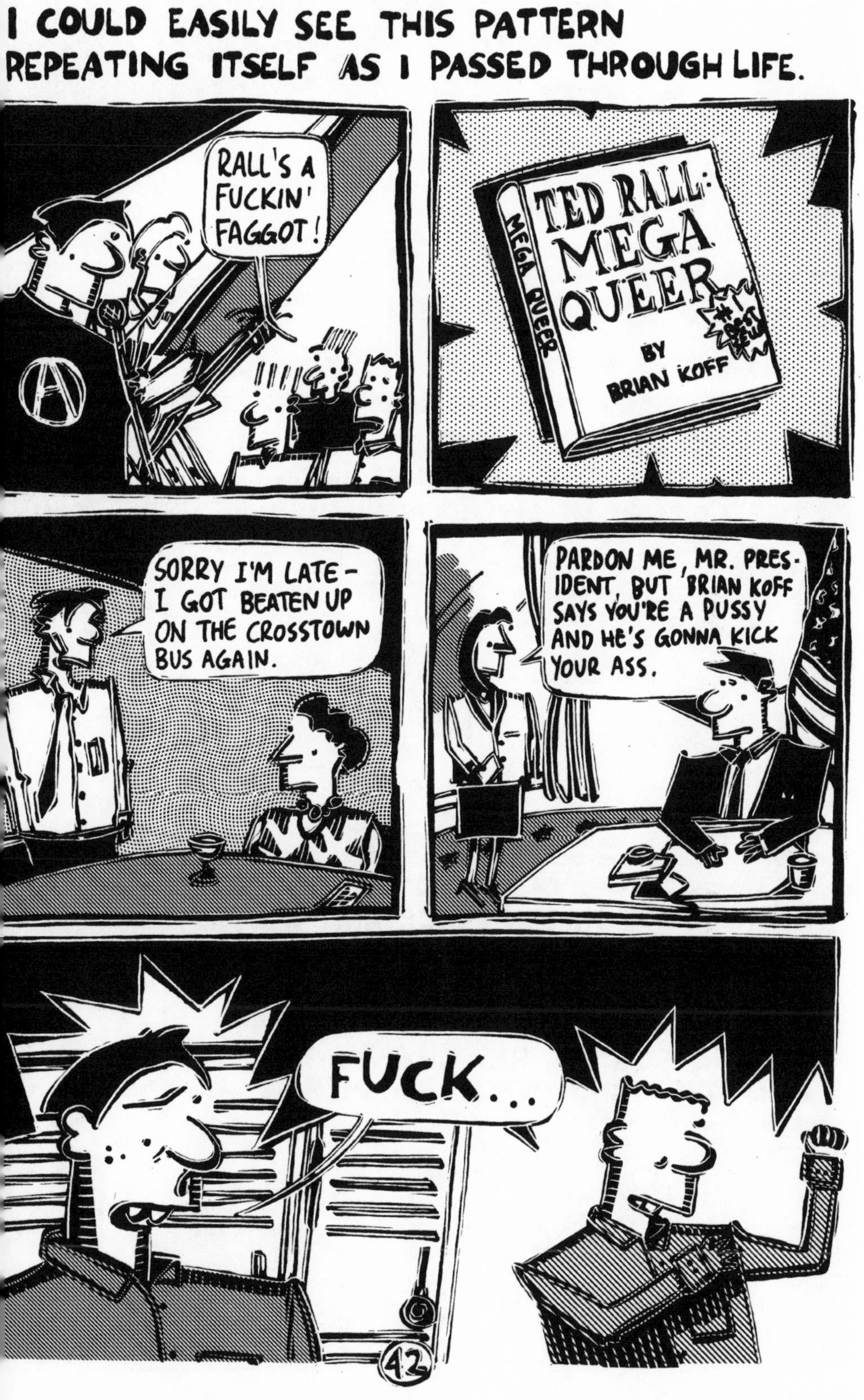
I COULD EASILY SEE THIS PATTERN REPEATING ITSELF AS I PASSED THROUGH LIFE.
RALL'S A FUCKIN' FAGGOT!
TED RALL: MEGA QUEER
MEGA QUEER
BY BRIAN KOFF
SORRY I'M LATE - I GOT BEATEN UP ON THE CROSSTOWN BUS AGAIN.
PARDON ME, MR. PRESIDENT, BUT BRIAN KOFF SAYS YOU'RE A PUSSY AND HE'S GONNA KICK YOUR ASS.
FUCK...

I GRABBED KOFF'S HEAD BY HIS HAIR AND SLAMMED IT INTO THE CORNER OF MY OPEN LOCKER.

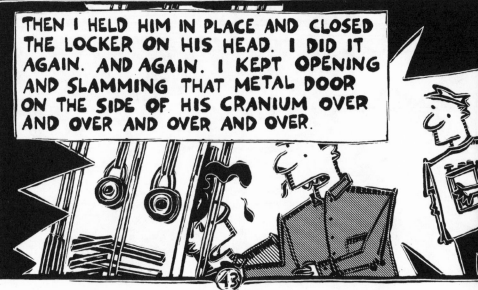

THEN I HELD HIM IN PLACE AND CLOSED THE LOCKER ON HIS HEAD. I DID IT AGAIN. AND AGAIN. I KEPT OPENING AND SLAMMING THAT METAL DOOR ON THE SIDE OF HIS CRANIUM OVER AND OVER AND OVER AND OVER.

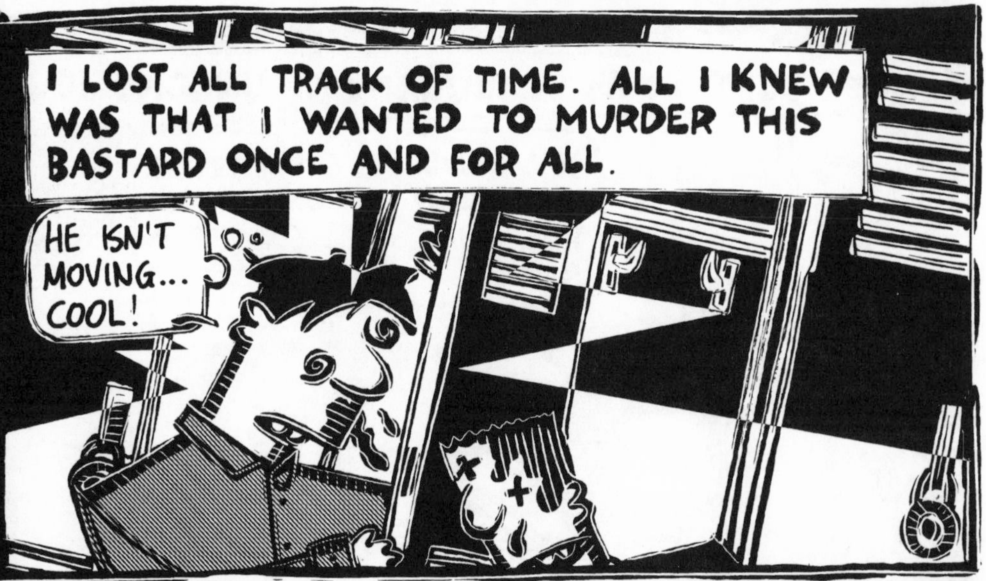
I LOST ALL TRACK OF TIME. ALL I KNEW WAS THAT I WANTED TO MURDER THIS BASTARD ONCE AND FOR ALL.
HE ISN'T MOVING... COOL!

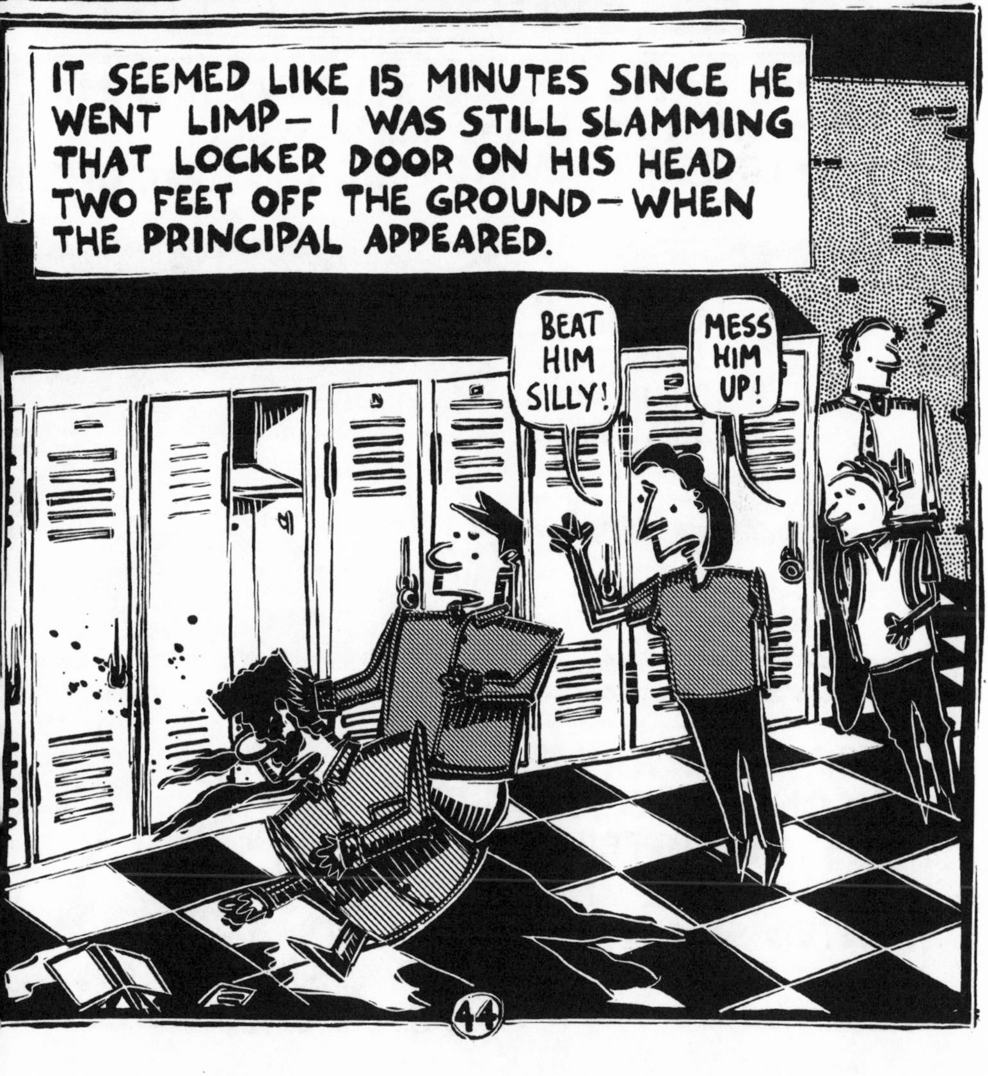
IT SEEMED LIKE 15 MINUTES SINCE HE WENT LIMP— I WAS STILL SLAMMING THAT LOCKER DOOR ON HIS HEAD TWO FEET OFF THE GROUND—WHEN THE PRINCIPAL APPEARED.
BEAT HIM SILLY!
MESS HIM UP!
?

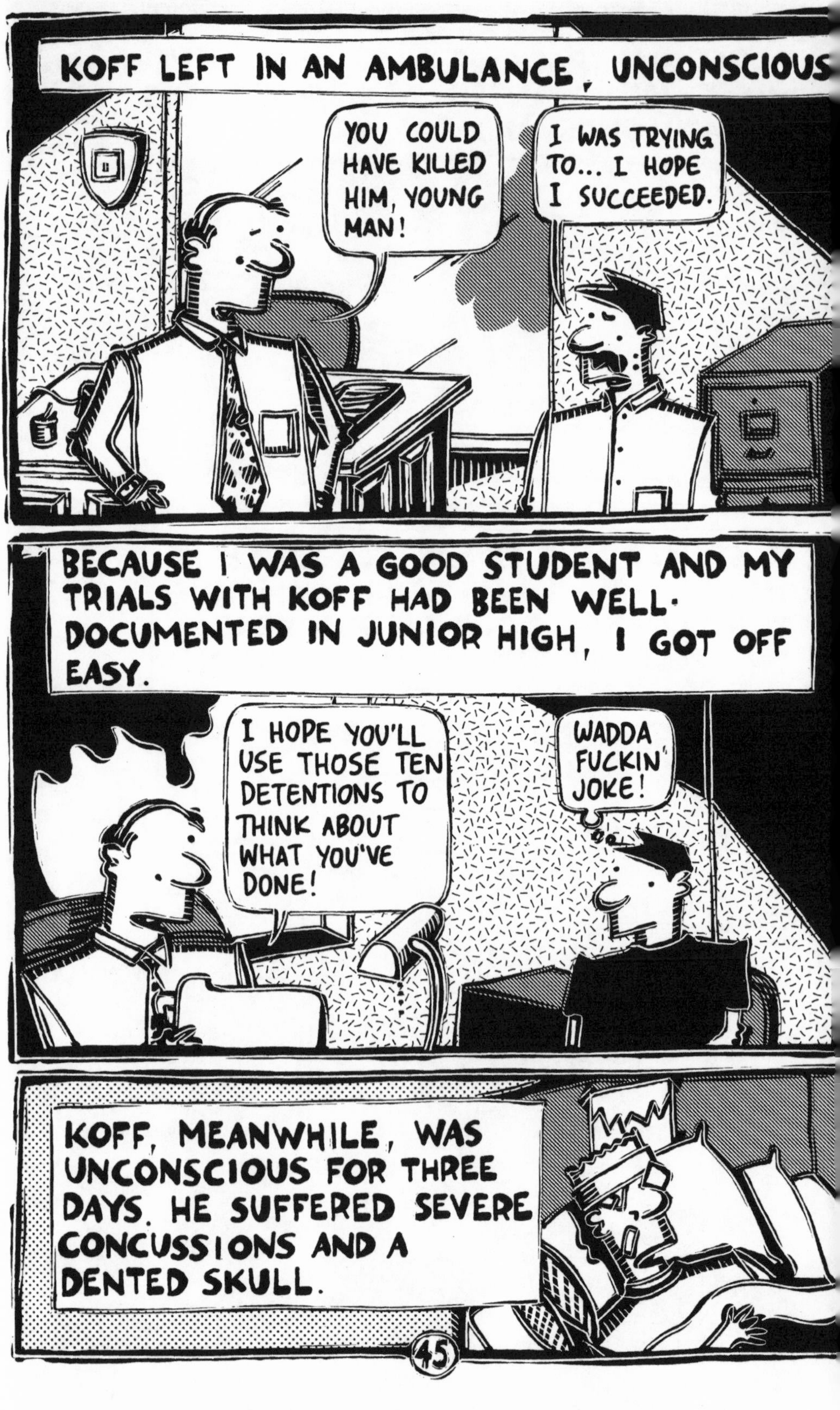
KOFF LEFT IN AN AMBULANCE, UNCONSCIOUS
YOU COULD HAVE KILLED HIM, YOUNG MAN!
I WAS TRYING TO... I HOPE I SUCCEEDED.
BECAUSE I WAS A GOOD STUDENT AND MY TRIALS WITH KOFF HAD BEEN WELL-DOCUMENTED IN JUNIOR HIGH, I GOT OFF EASY.
I HOPE YOU'LL USE THOSE TEN DETENTIONS TO THINK ABOUT WHAT YOU'VE DONE!
WADDA FUCKIN' JOKE!
KOFF, MEANWHILE, WAS UNCONSCIOUS FOR THREE DAYS. HE SUFFERED SEVERE CONCUSSIONS AND A DENTED SKULL.

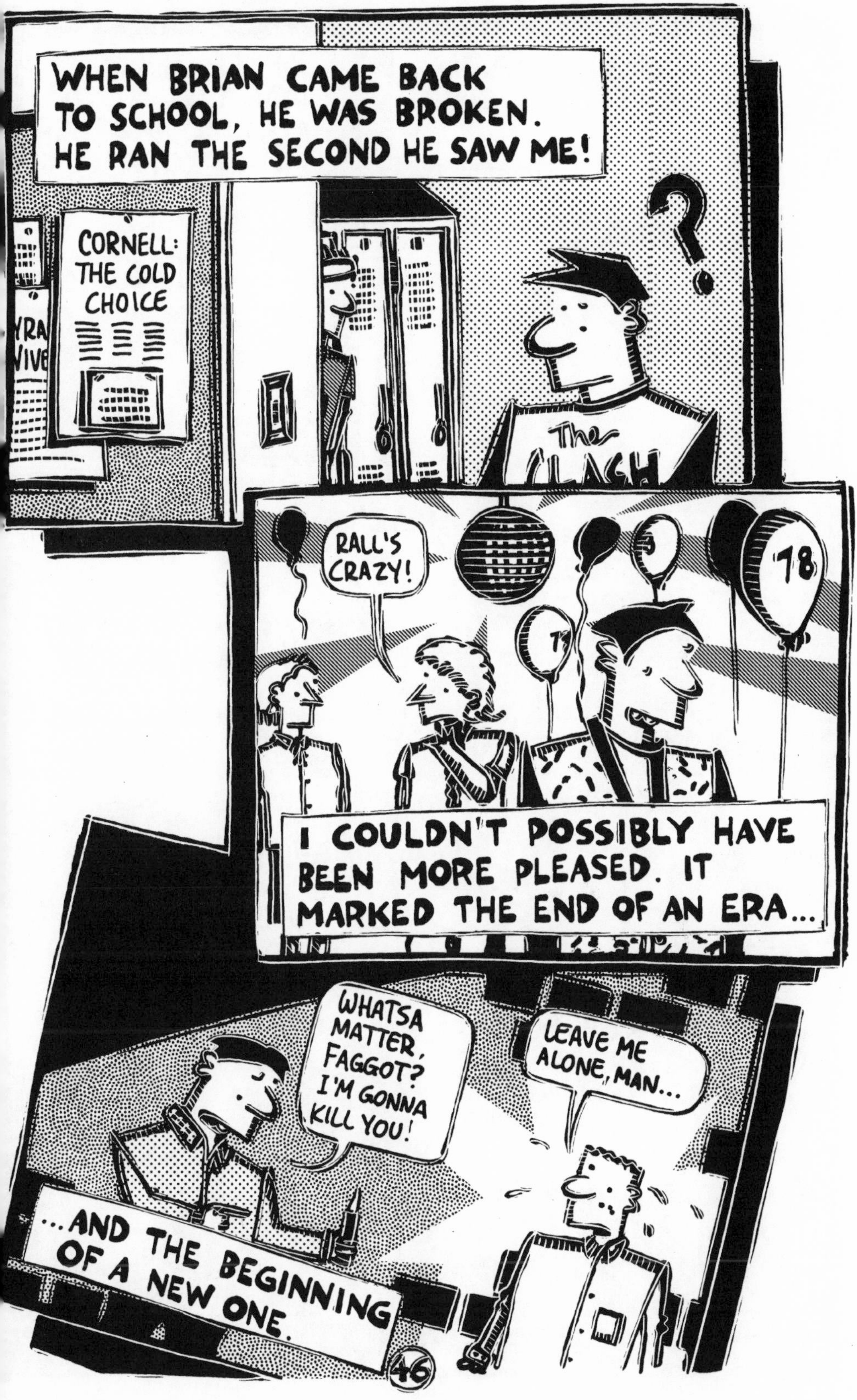
WHEN BRIAN CAME BACK TO SCHOOL, HE WAS BROKEN. HE RAN THE SECOND HE SAW ME!
CORNELL: THE COLD CHOICE
?
RALL'S CRAZY!
'78
I COULDN'T POSSIBLY HAVE BEEN MORE PLEASED. IT MARKED THE END OF AN ERA...
WHATSA MATTER, FAGGOT? I'M GONNA KILL YOU!
LEAVE ME ALONE, MAN...
...AND THE BEGINNING OF A NEW ONE.

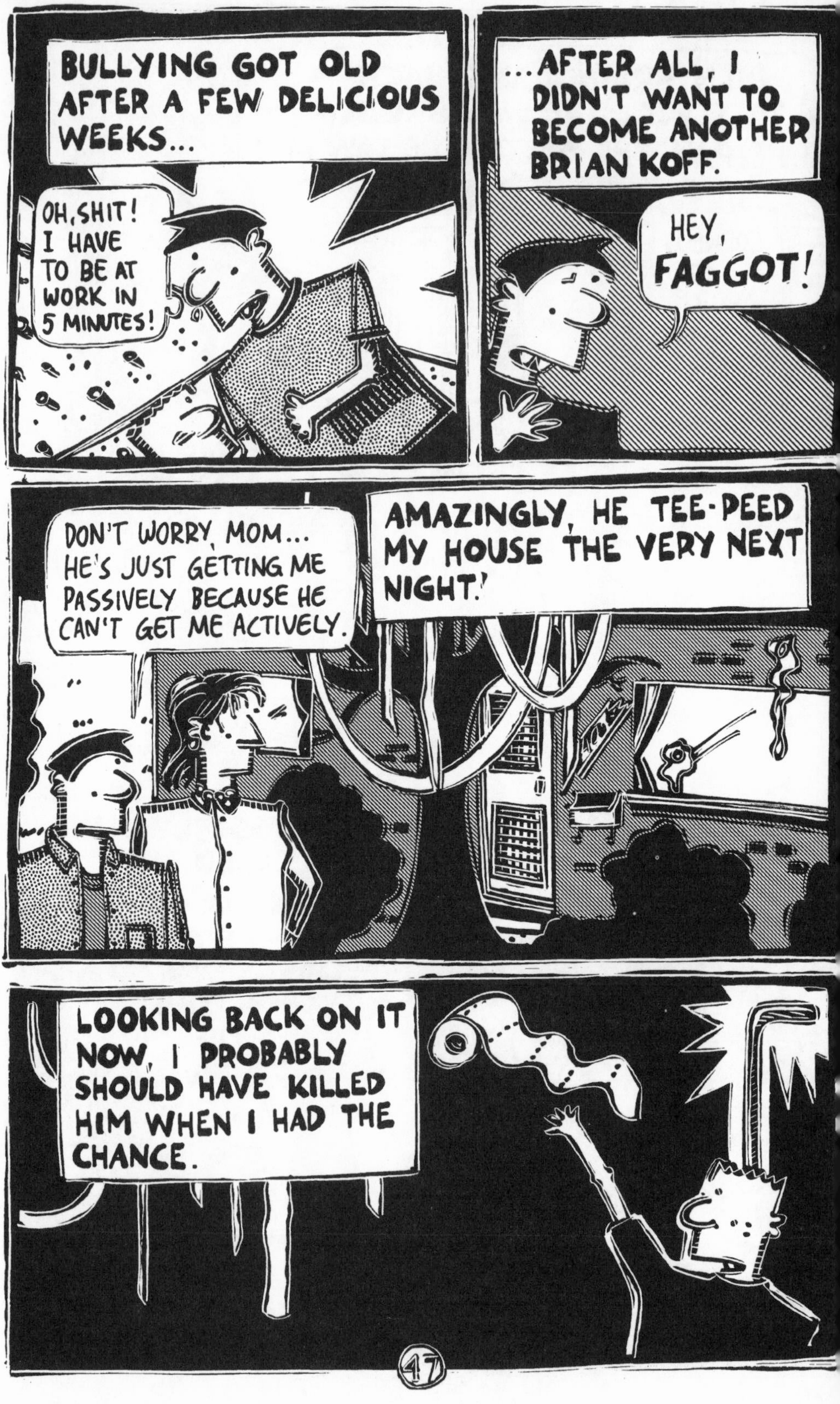

BULLYING GOT OLD AFTER A FEW DELICIOUS WEEKS...
OH, SHIT! I HAVE TO BE AT WORK IN 5 MINUTES!
...AFTER ALL, I DIDN'T WANT TO BECOME ANOTHER BRIAN KOFF.
HEY, FAGGOT!
DON'T WORRY, MOM... HE'S JUST GETTING ME PASSIVELY BECAUSE HE CAN'T GET ME ACTIVELY.
AMAZINGLY, HE TEE-PEED MY HOUSE THE VERY NEXT NIGHT.
...
LOOKING BACK ON IT NOW, I PROBABLY SHOULD HAVE KILLED HIM WHEN I HAD THE CHANCE.

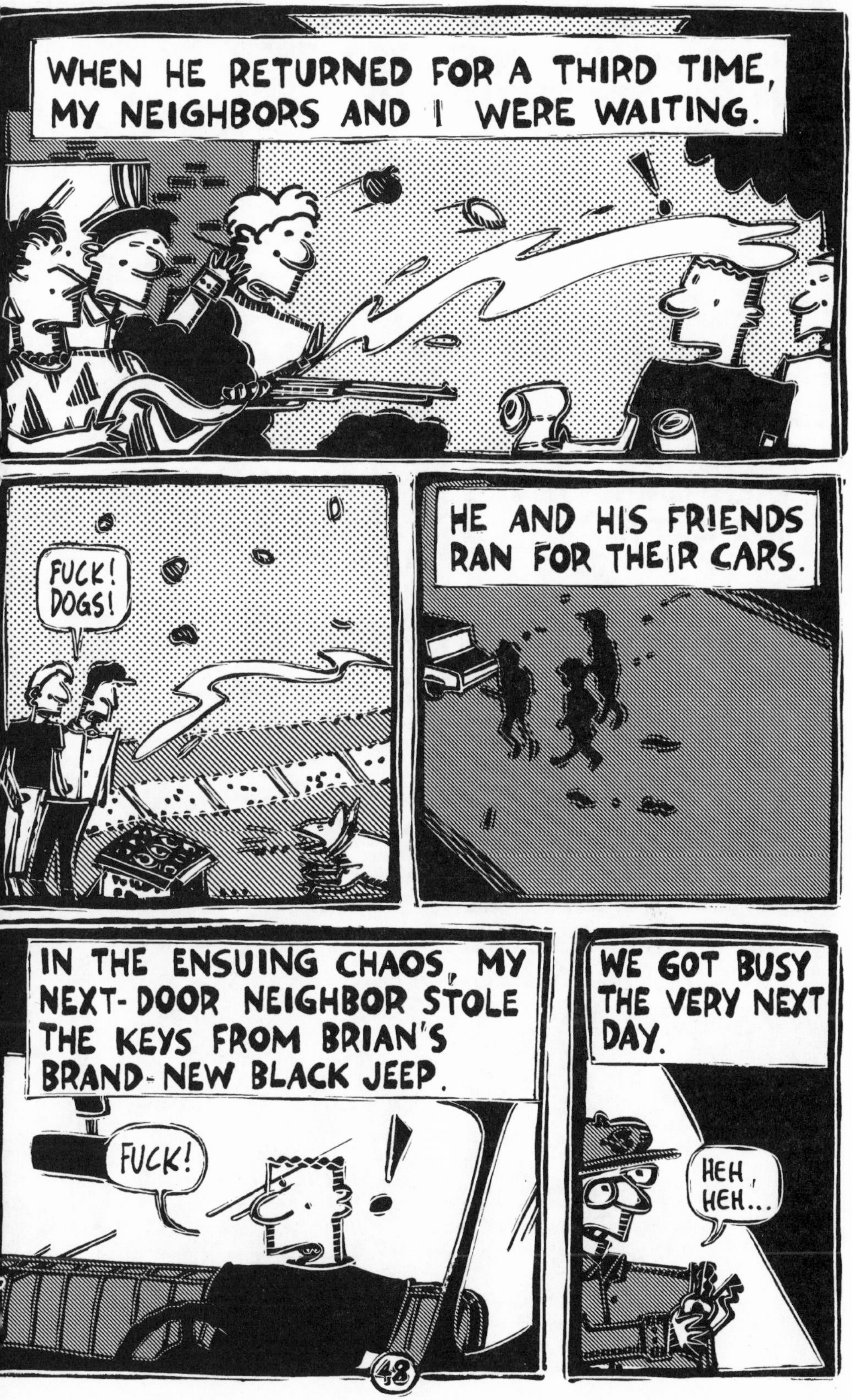
WHEN HE RETURNED FOR A THIRD TIME, MY NEIGHBORS AND I WERE WAITING.
FUCK! DOGS!
HE AND HIS FRIENDS RAN FOR THEIR CARS.
IN THE ENSUING CHAOS, MY NEXT-DOOR NEIGHBOR STOLE THE KEYS FROM BRIAN'S BRAND-NEW BLACK JEEP.
FUCK!
WE GOT BUSY THE VERY NEXT DAY.
HEH, HEH...

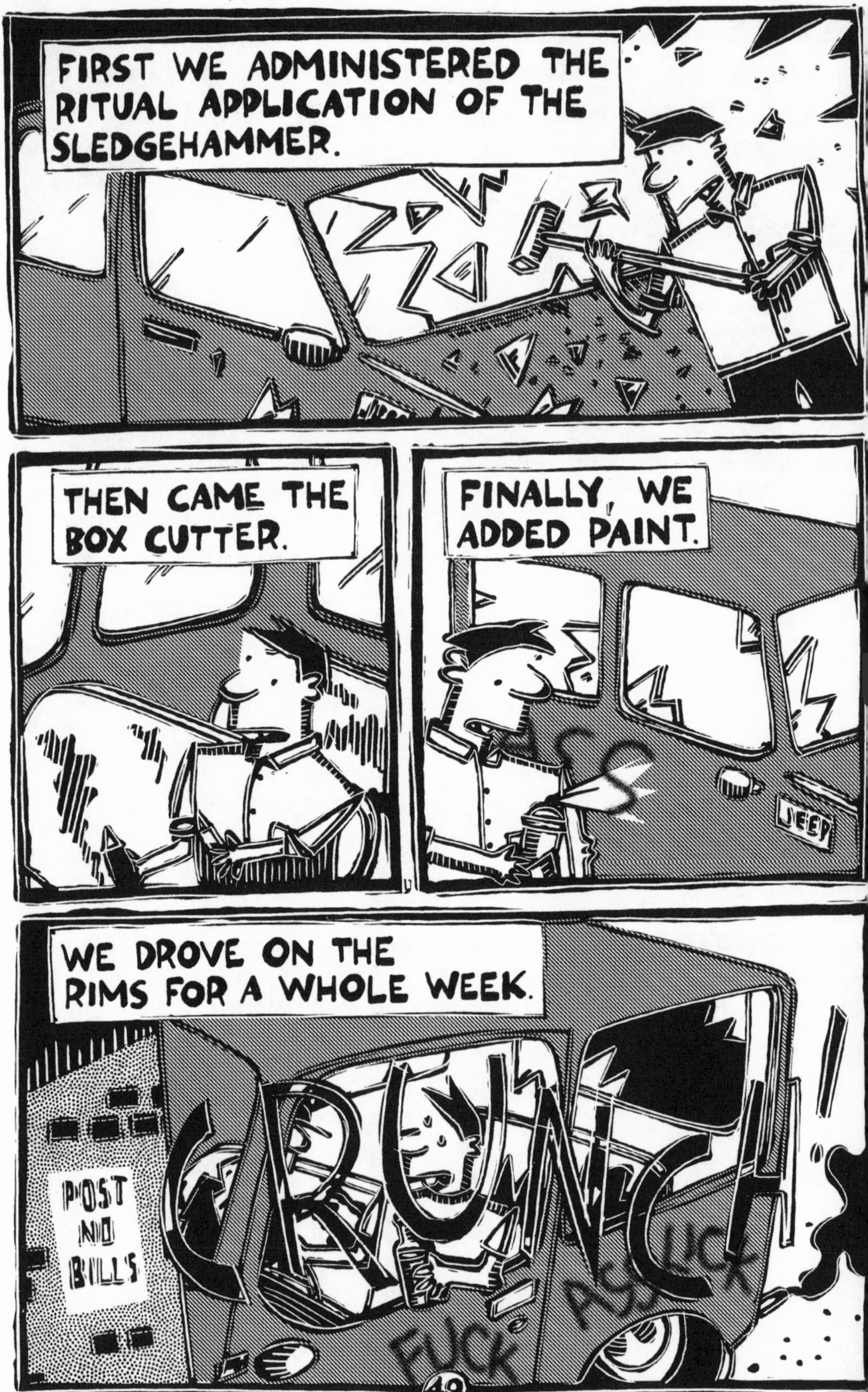
FIRST WE ADMINISTERED THE RITUAL APPLICATION OF THE SLEDGEHAMMER.
THEN CAME THE BOX CUTTER.
FINALLY, WE ADDED PAINT.
ASS
JEEP
WE DROVE ON THE RIMS FOR A WHOLE WEEK.
CRUNCH!
POST NO BILLS
FUCK
ASS

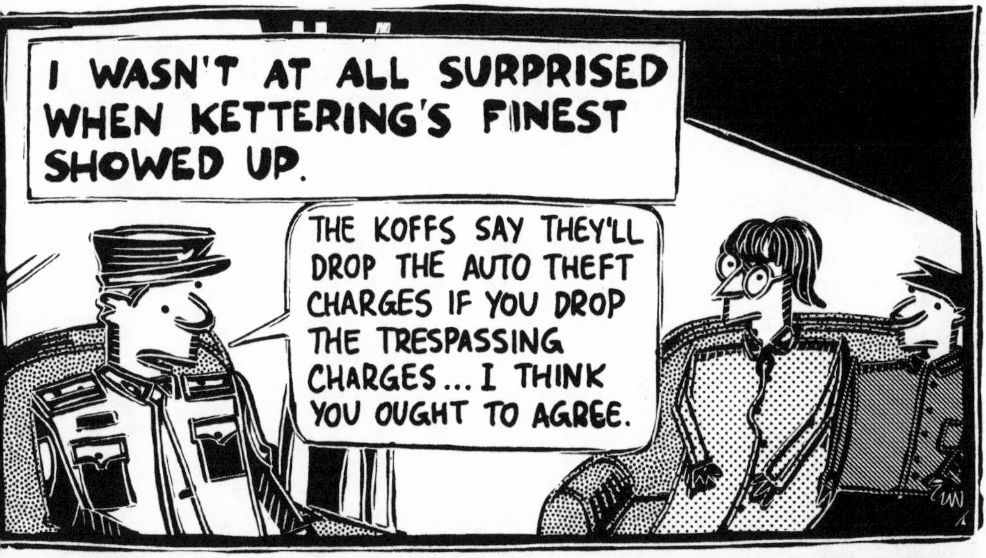
I WASN'T AT ALL SURPRISED WHEN KETTERING'S FINEST SHOWED UP.
THE KOFFS SAY THEY'LL DROP THE AUTO THEFT CHARGES IF YOU DROP THE TRESPASSING CHARGES... I THINK YOU OUGHT TO AGREE.

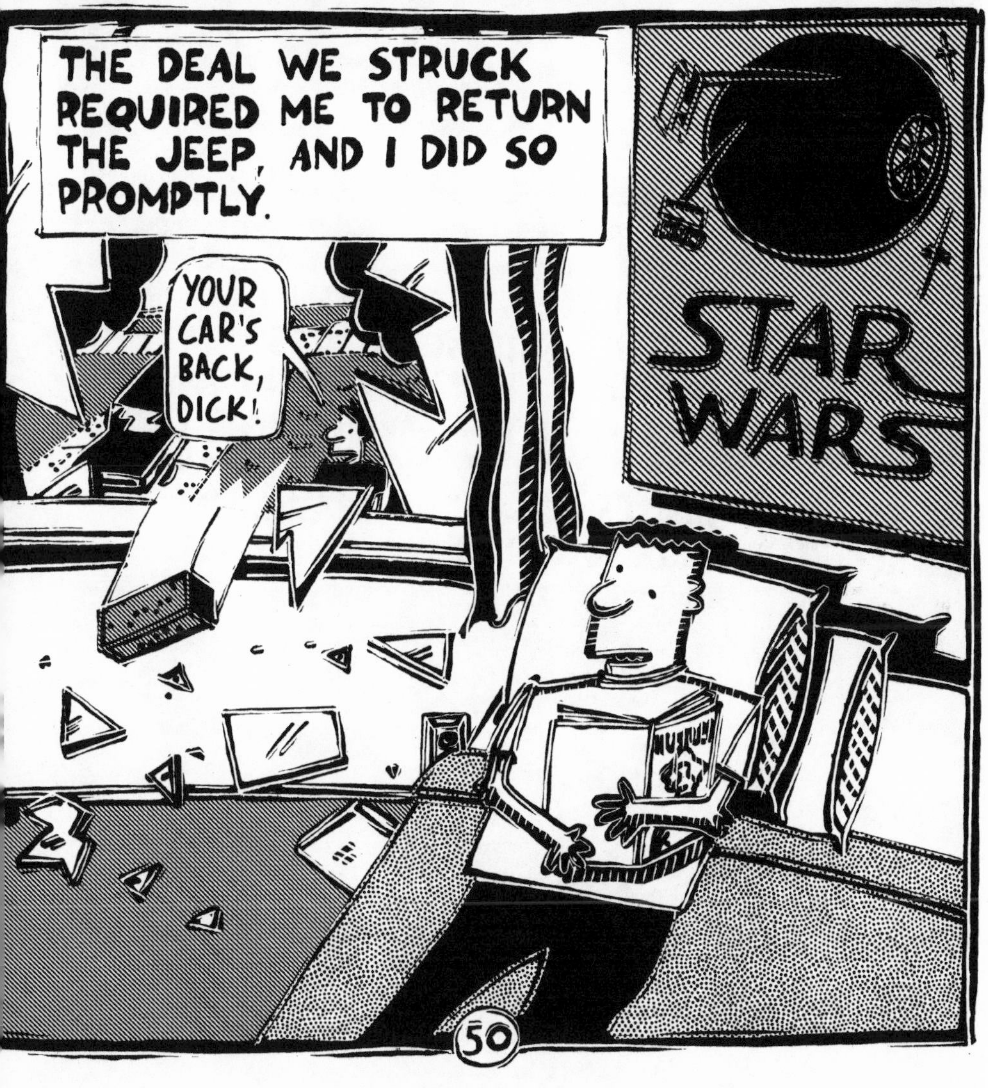
THE DEAL WE STRUCK REQUIRED ME TO RETURN THE JEEP, AND I DID SO PROMPTLY.
YOUR CAR'S BACK, DICK!
STAR WARS

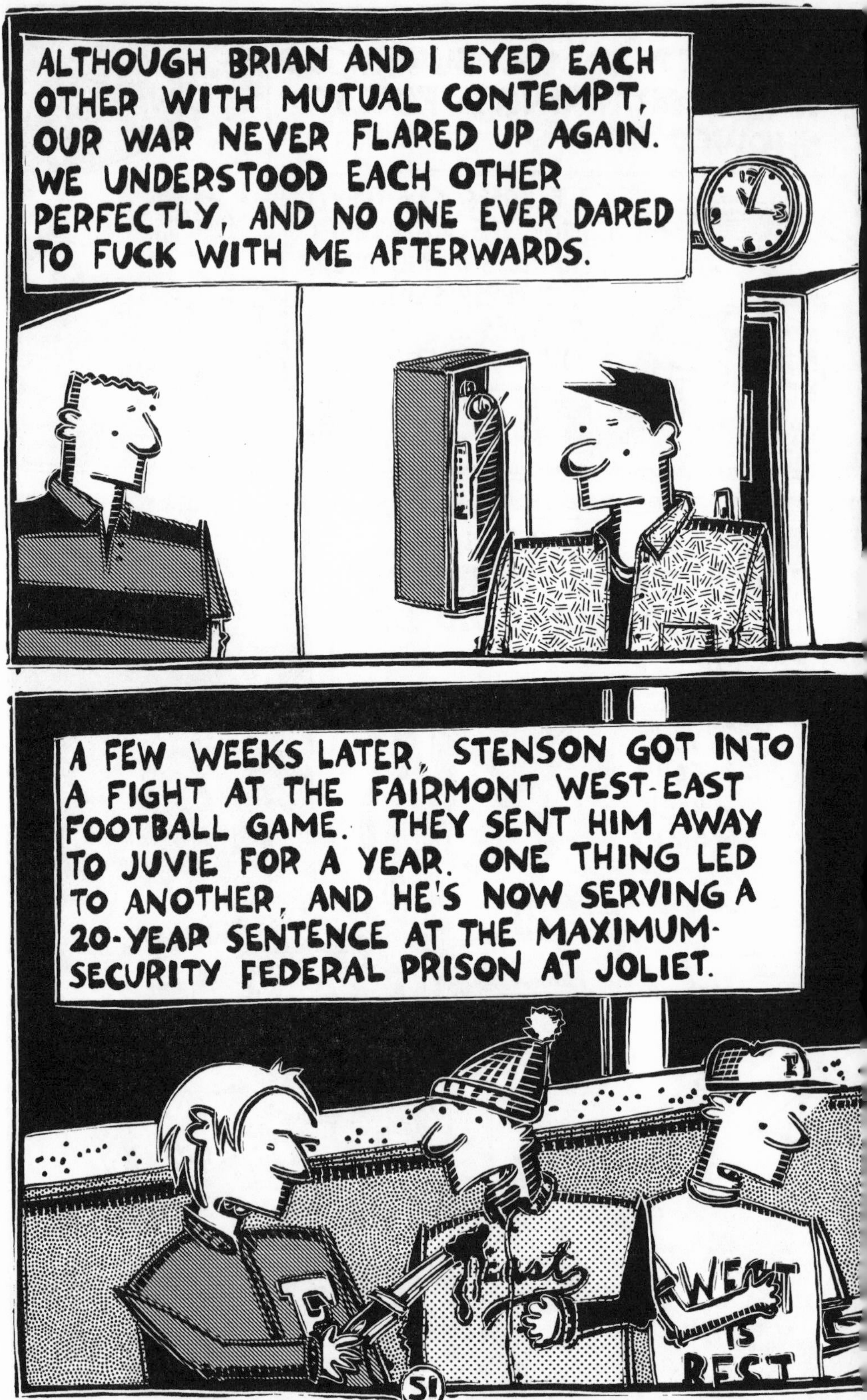
ALTHOUGH BRIAN AND I EYED EACH OTHER WITH MUTUAL CONTEMPT, OUR WAR NEVER FLARED UP AGAIN. WE UNDERSTOOD EACH OTHER PERFECTLY, AND NO ONE EVER DARED TO FUCK WITH ME AFTERWARDS.
A FEW WEEKS LATER, STENSON GOT INTO A FIGHT AT THE FAIRMONT WEST-EAST FOOTBALL GAME. THEY SENT HIM AWAY TO JUVIE FOR A YEAR. ONE THING LED TO ANOTHER, AND HE'S NOW SERVING A 20-YEAR SENTENCE AT THE MAXIMUM-SECURITY FEDERAL PRISON AT JOLIET.
East
WEST
IS

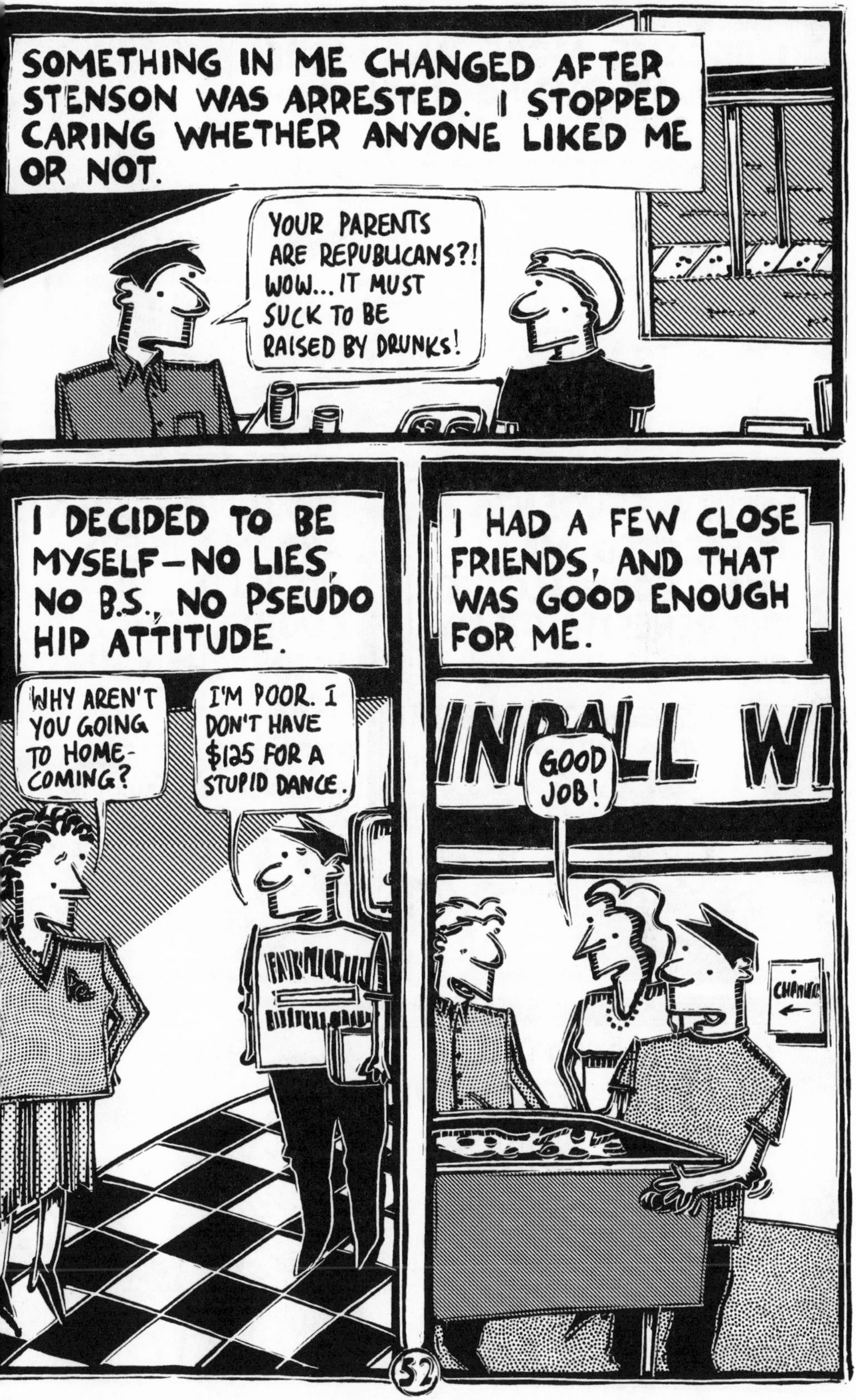

SOMETHING IN ME CHANGED AFTER STENSON WAS ARRESTED. I STOPPED CARING WHETHER ANYONE LIKED ME OR NOT.
YOUR PARENTS ARE REPUBLICANS?! WOW... IT MUST SUCK TO BE RAISED BY DRUNKS!
I DECIDED TO BE MYSELF—NO LIES, NO B.S., NO PSEUDO HIP ATTITUDE.
WHY AREN'T YOU GOING TO HOME-COMING?
I'M POOR. I DON'T HAVE $125 FOR A STUPID DANCE.
I HAD A FEW CLOSE FRIENDS, AND THAT WAS GOOD ENOUGH FOR ME.
INBALL WI
GOOD JOB!

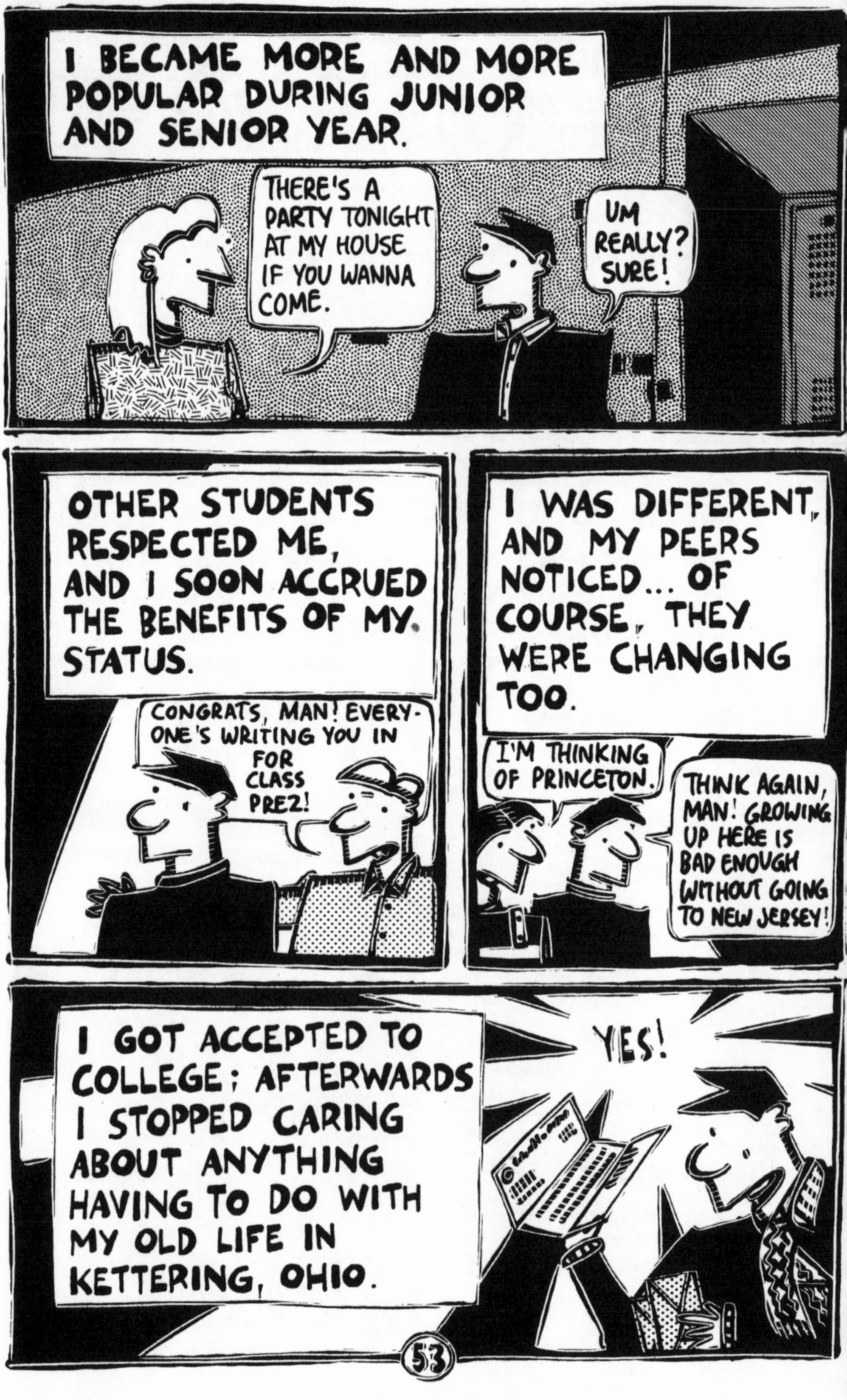
I BECAME MORE AND MORE POPULAR DURING JUNIOR AND SENIOR YEAR.
THERE'S A PARTY TONIGHT AT MY HOUSE IF YOU WANNA COME.
UM REALLY? SURE!
OTHER STUDENTS RESPECTED ME, AND I SOON ACCRUED THE BENEFITS OF MY STATUS.
CONGRATS, MAN! EVERYONE'S WRITING YOU IN FOR CLASS PREZ!
I WAS DIFFERENT, AND MY PEERS NOTICED... OF COURSE, THEY WERE CHANGING TOO.
I'M THINKING OF PRINCETON.
THINK AGAIN, MAN! GROWING UP HERE IS BAD ENOUGH WITHOUT GOING TO NEW JERSEY!
I GOT ACCEPTED TO COLLEGE; AFTERWARDS I STOPPED CARING ABOUT ANYTHING HAVING TO DO WITH MY OLD LIFE IN KETTERING, OHIO.
YES!

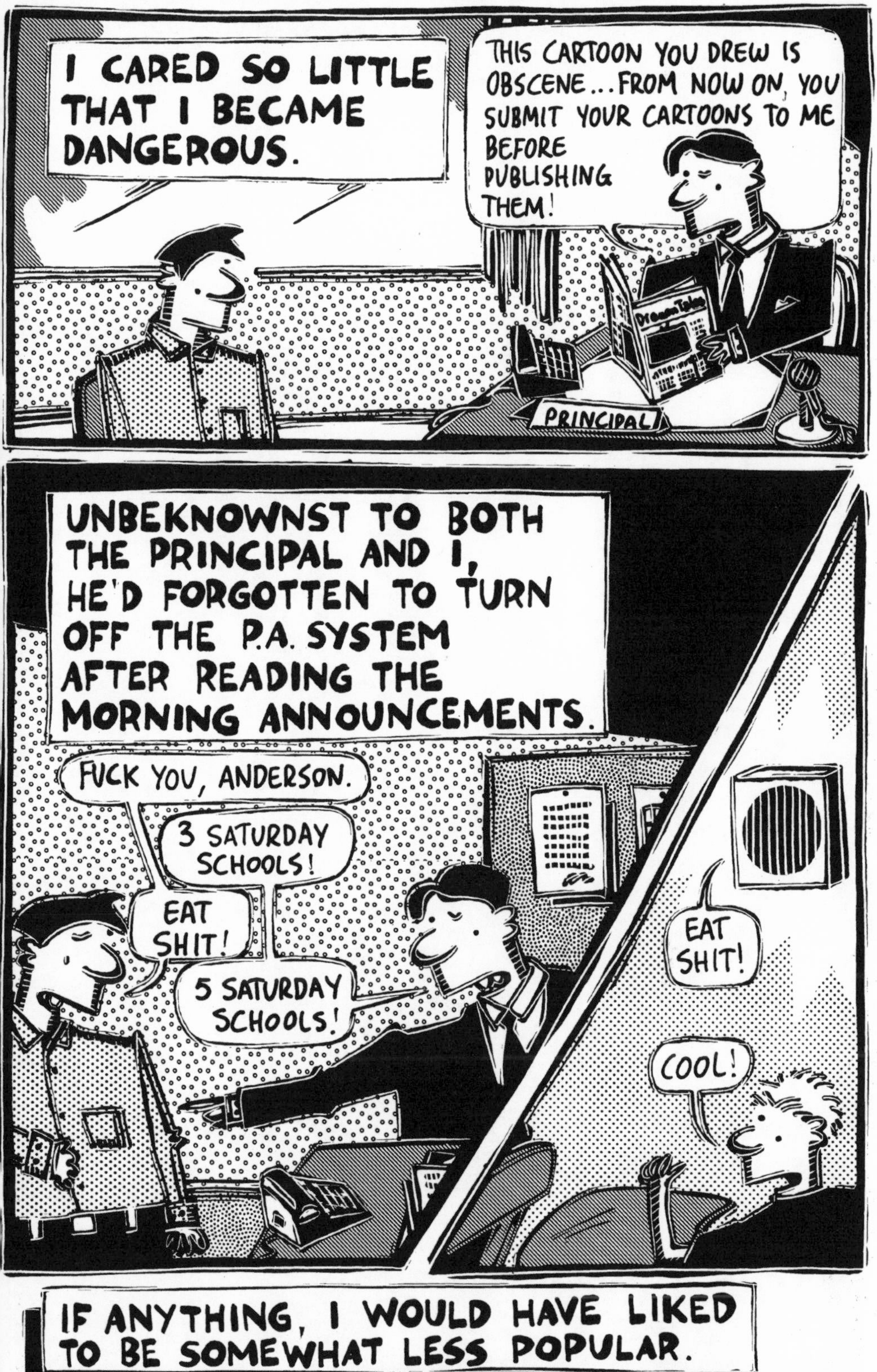
I CARED SO LITTLE THAT I BECAME DANGEROUS.
THIS CARTOON YOU DREW IS OBSCENE... FROM NOW ON, YOU SUBMIT YOUR CARTOONS TO ME BEFORE PUBLISHING THEM!
PRINCIPAL
UNBEKNOWNST TO BOTH THE PRINCIPAL AND I, HE'D FORGOTTEN TO TURN OFF THE P.A. SYSTEM AFTER READING THE MORNING ANNOUNCEMENTS.
FUCK YOU, ANDERSON.
3 SATURDAY SCHOOLS!
EAT SHIT!
5 SATURDAY SCHOOLS!
EAT SHIT!
COOL!
IF ANYTHING, I WOULD HAVE LIKED TO BE SOMEWHAT LESS POPULAR.

-7-
COMMENCEMENT

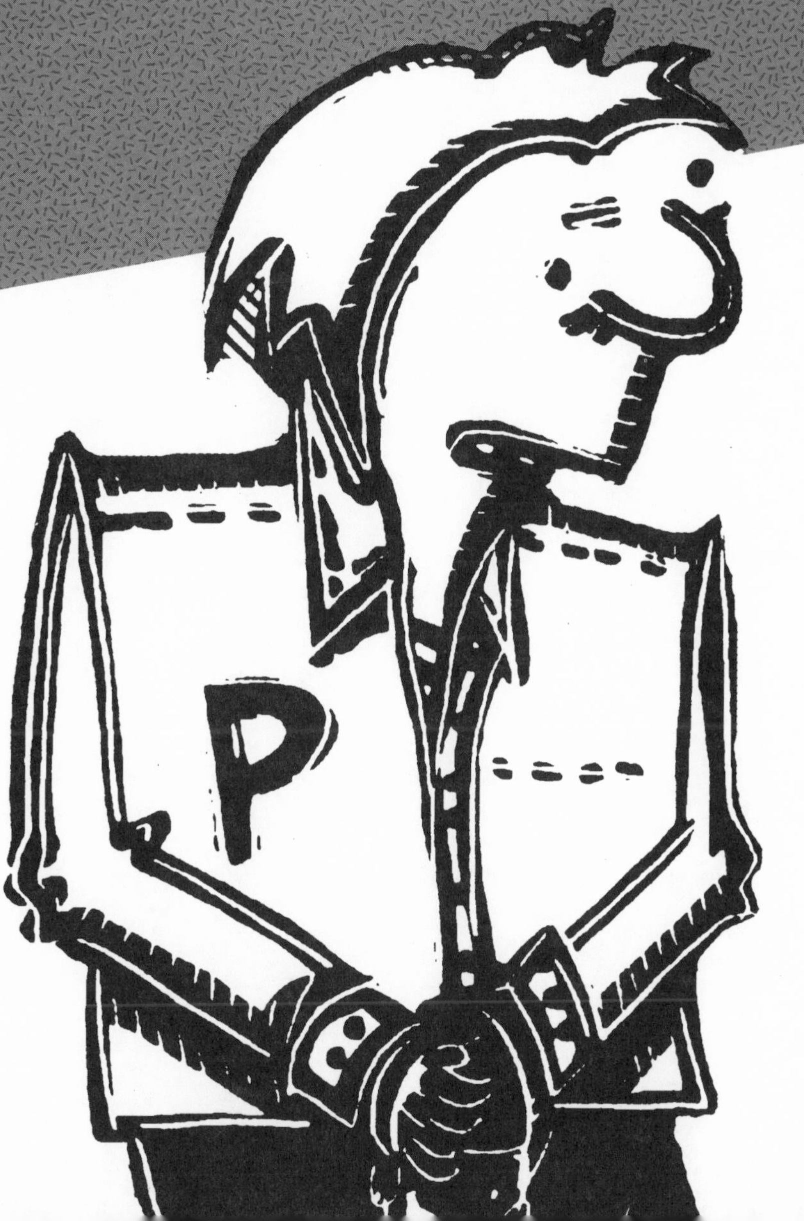
P

MY WAR WITH BRIAN TURNED OUT TO BE A PRECURSOR TO HUNDREDS OF CONFLICTS WITH PEOPLE WHO EQUATED MY REASONABLE DEMEANOR WITH WEAKNESS.

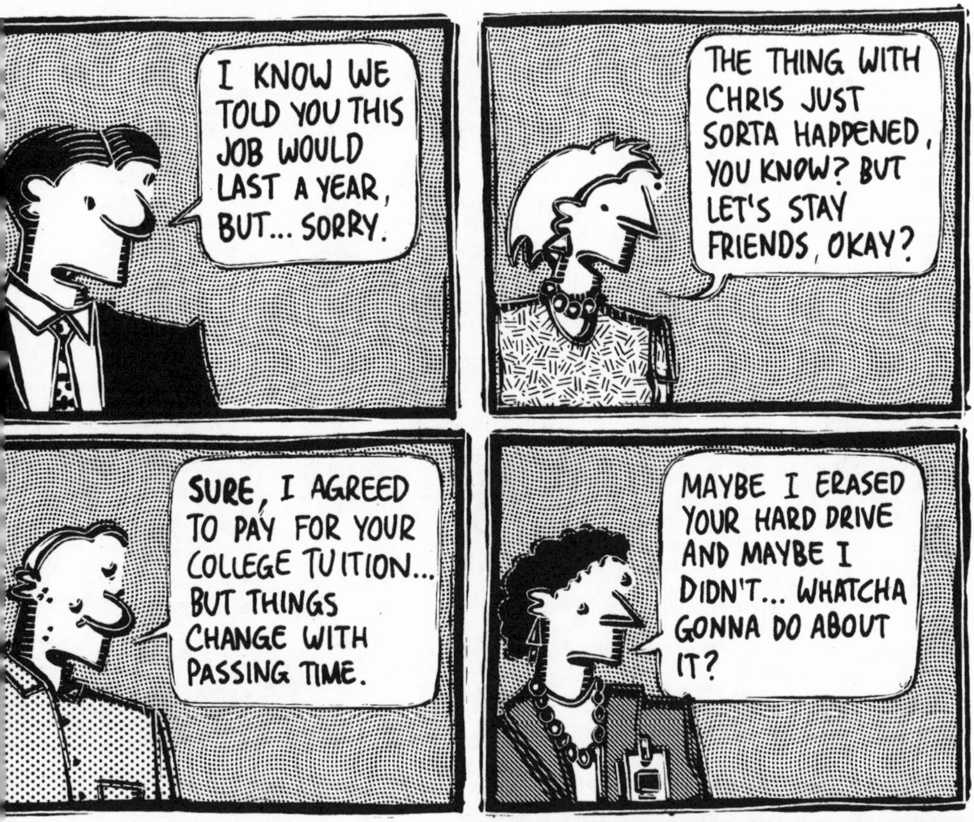
I KNOW WE TOLD YOU THIS JOB WOULD LAST A YEAR, BUT... SORRY.
THE THING WITH CHRIS JUST SORTA HAPPENED, YOU KNOW? BUT LET'S STAY FRIENDS, OKAY?
SURE, I AGREED TO PAY FOR YOUR COLLEGE TUITION... BUT THINGS CHANGE WITH PASSING TIME.
MAYBE I ERASED YOUR HARD DRIVE AND MAYBE I DIDN'T... WHATCHA GONNA DO ABOUT IT?

FORTUNATELY, HE TAUGHT ME THAT EVERY OFFENSE MUST BE MET WITH A REACTION TWICE AS FIERCE, EVEN IF IT MEANS SHORT-TERM SUFFERING.

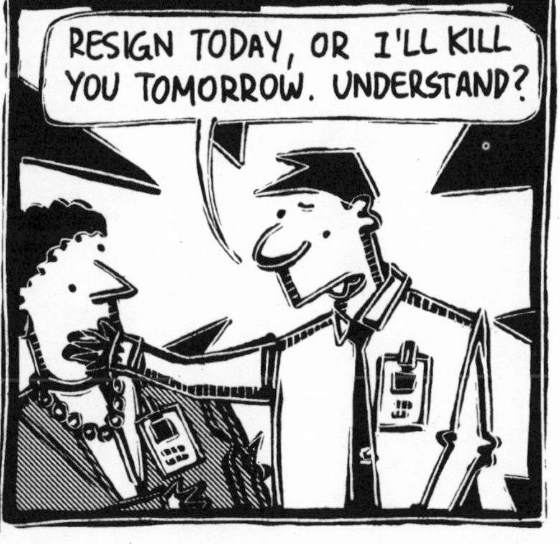
RESIGN TODAY, OR I'LL KILL YOU TOMORROW. UNDERSTAND?

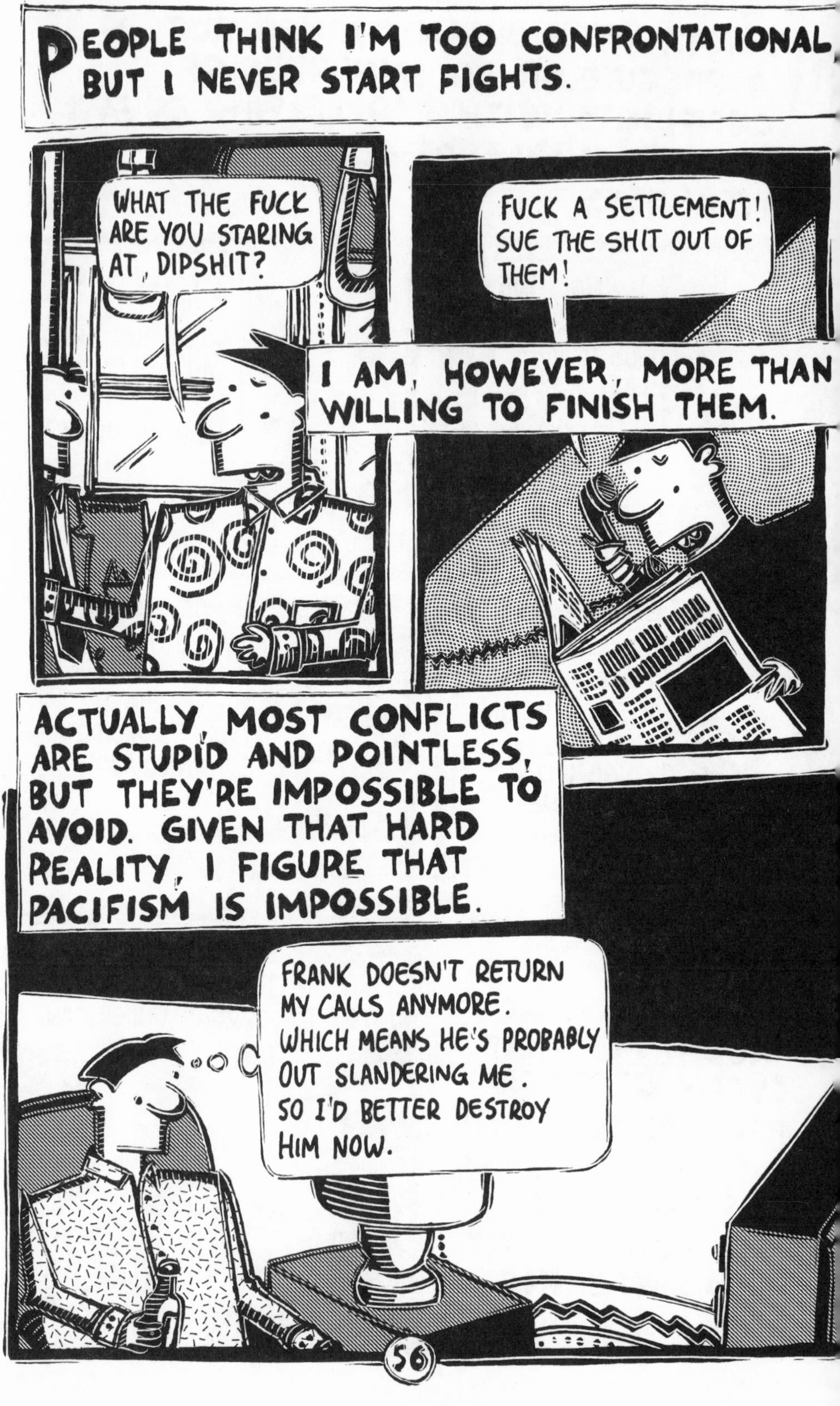
PEOPLE THINK I'M TOO CONFRONTATIONAL, BUT I NEVER START FIGHTS.
WHAT THE FUCK ARE YOU STARING AT, DIPSHIT?
FUCK A SETTLEMENT! SUE THE SHIT OUT OF THEM!
I AM, HOWEVER, MORE THAN WILLING TO FINISH THEM.
ACTUALLY, MOST CONFLICTS ARE STUPID AND POINTLESS, BUT THEY'RE IMPOSSIBLE TO AVOID. GIVEN THAT HARD REALITY, I FIGURE THAT PACIFISM IS IMPOSSIBLE.
FRANK DOESN'T RETURN MY CALLS ANYMORE. WHICH MEANS HE'S PROBABLY OUT SLANDERING ME. SO I'D BETTER DESTROY HIM NOW.

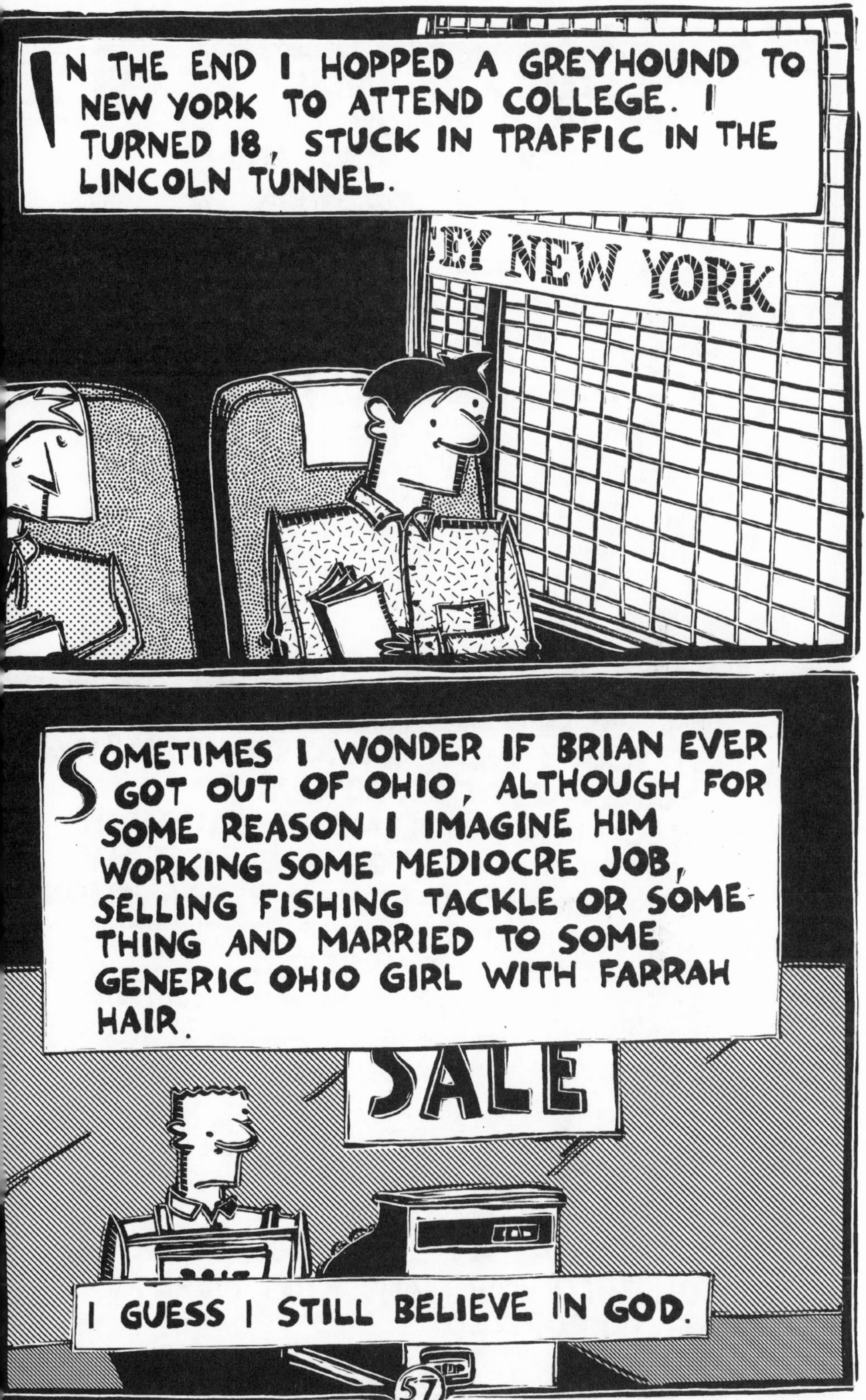
IN THE END I HOPPED A GREYHOUND TO NEW YORK TO ATTEND COLLEGE. I TURNED 18, STUCK IN TRAFFIC IN THE LINCOLN TUNNEL.
NEW YORK
SOMETIMES I WONDER IF BRIAN EVER GOT OUT OF OHIO, ALTHOUGH FOR SOME REASON I IMAGINE HIM WORKING SOME MEDIOCRE JOB, SELLING FISHING TACKLE OR SOME-THING AND MARRIED TO SOME GENERIC OHIO GIRL WITH FARRAH HAIR.
SALE
I GUESS I STILL BELIEVE IN GOD.

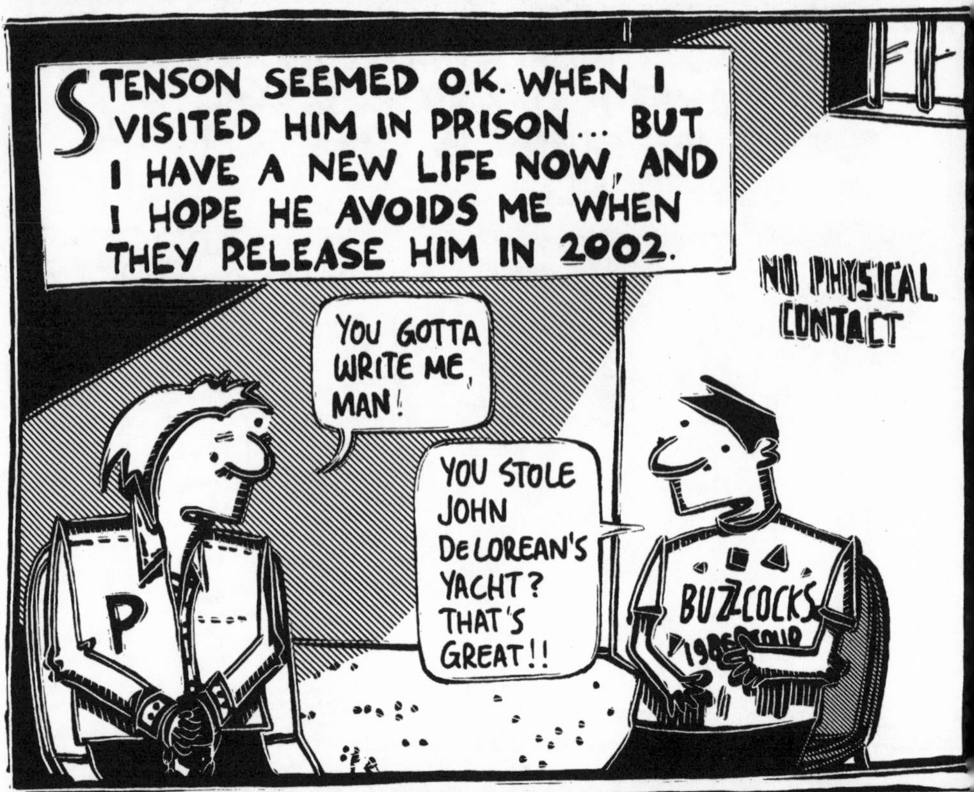
STENSON SEEMED O.K. WHEN I VISITED HIM IN PRISON... BUT I HAVE A NEW LIFE NOW, AND I HOPE HE AVOIDS ME WHEN THEY RELEASE HIM IN 2002.
NO PHYSICAL CONTACT
YOU GOTTA WRITE ME, MAN!
YOU STOLE JOHN DeLOREAN'S YACHT? THAT'S GREAT!!
P
BUZZCOCKS

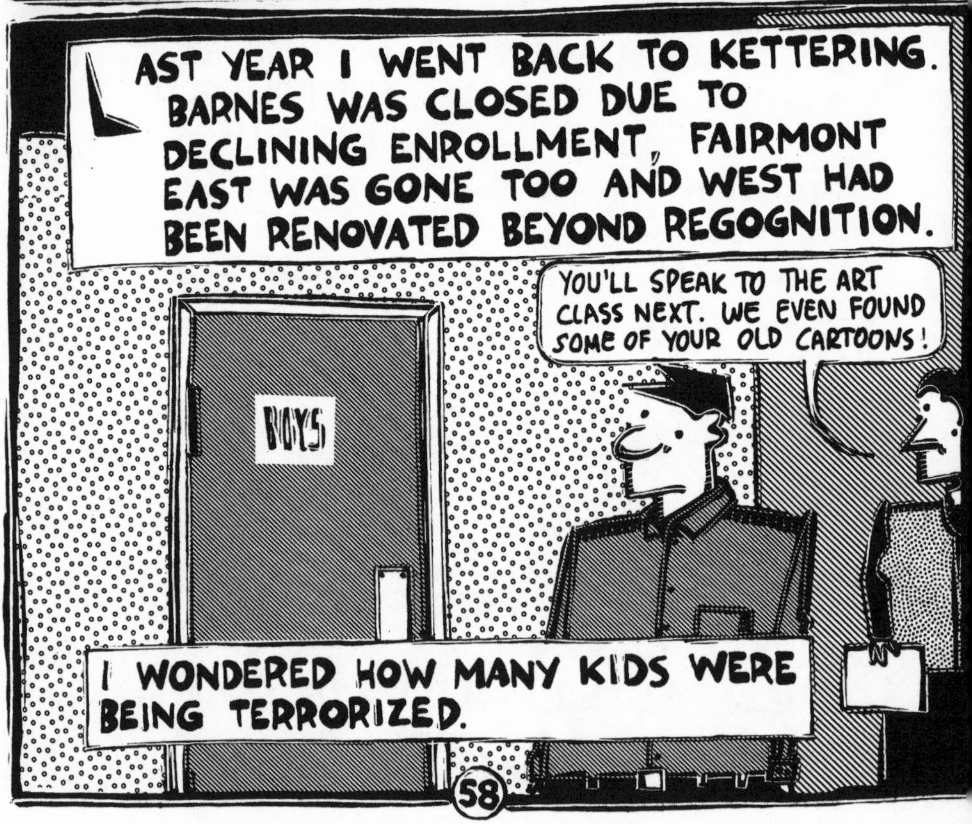
LAST YEAR I WENT BACK TO KETTERING. BARNES WAS CLOSED DUE TO DECLINING ENROLLMENT, FAIRMONT EAST WAS GONE TOO AND WEST HAD BEEN RENOVATED BEYOND REGOGNITION.
YOU'LL SPEAK TO THE ART CLASS NEXT. WE EVEN FOUND SOME OF YOUR OLD CARTOONS!
BOYS
I WONDERED HOW MANY KIDS WERE BEING TERRORIZED.

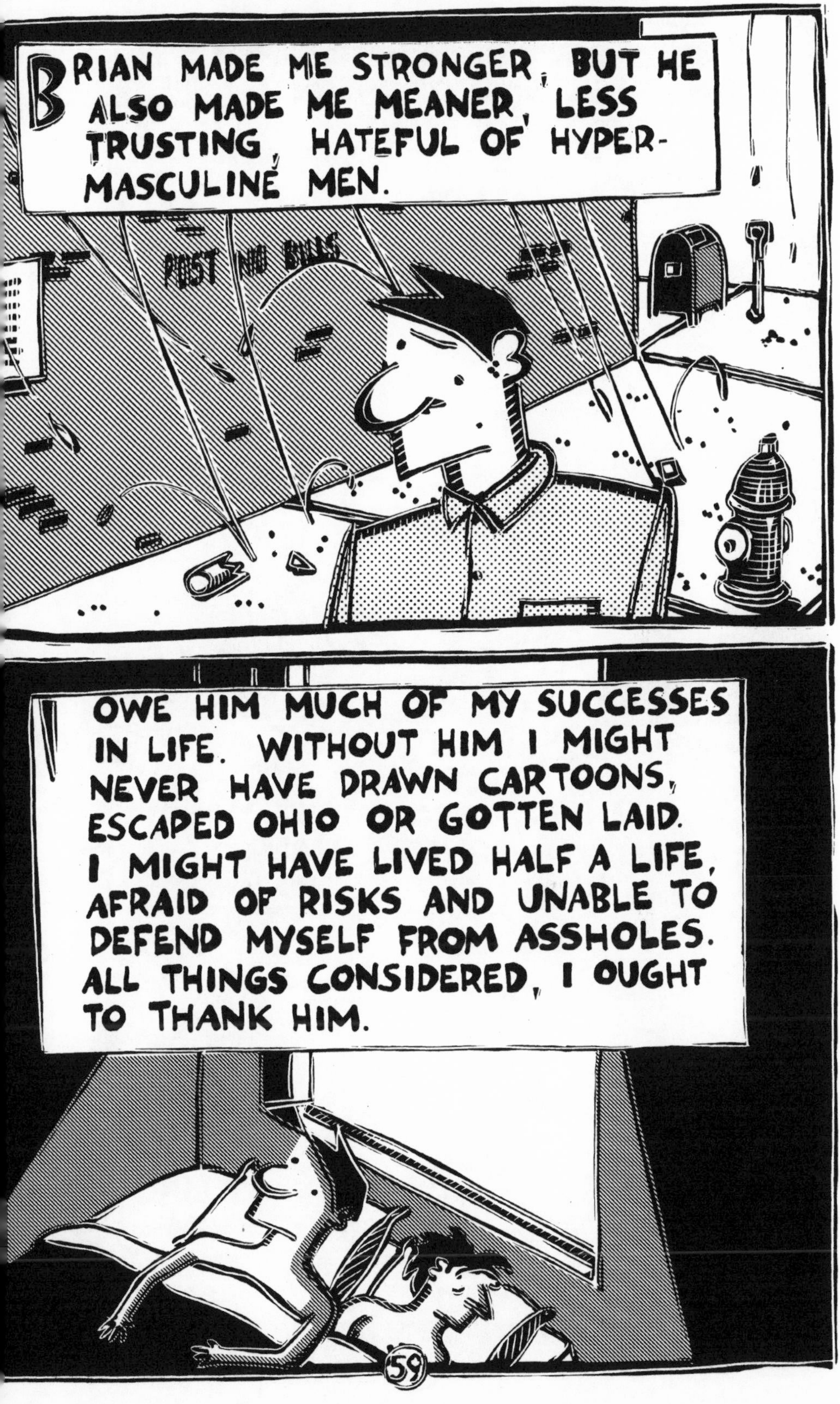
BRIAN MADE ME STRONGER, BUT HE ALSO MADE ME MEANER, LESS TRUSTING, HATEFUL OF HYPER-MASCULINE MEN.
POST NO BILLS
I OWE HIM MUCH OF MY SUCCESSES IN LIFE. WITHOUT HIM I MIGHT NEVER HAVE DRAWN CARTOONS, ESCAPED OHIO OR GOTTEN LAID. I MIGHT HAVE LIVED HALF A LIFE, AFRAID OF RISKS AND UNABLE TO DEFEND MYSELF FROM ASSHOLES. ALL THINGS CONSIDERED, I OUGHT TO THANK HIM.

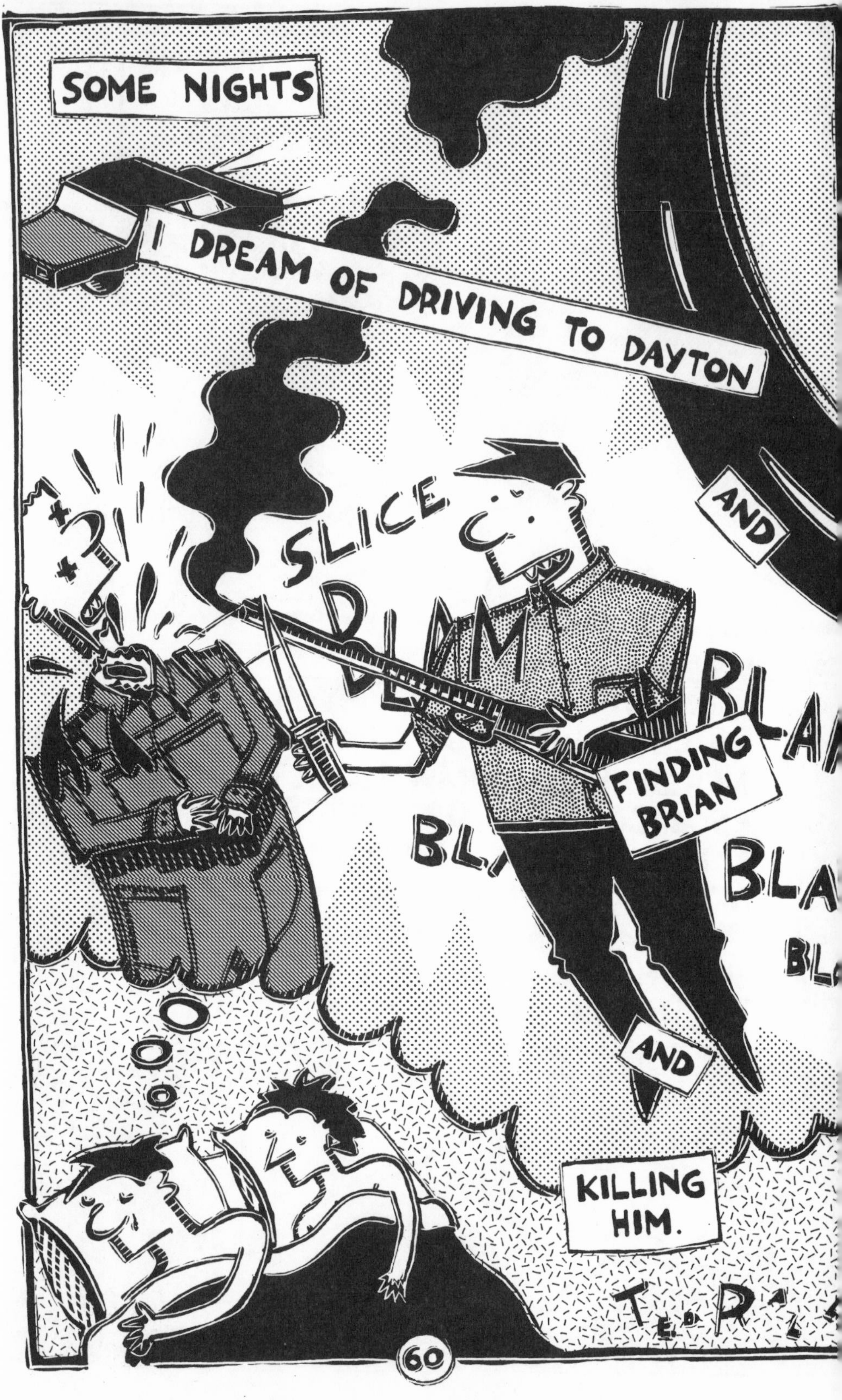
SOME NIGHTS
I DREAM OF DRIVING TO DAYTON
AND
SLICE
FINDING BRIAN
AND
KILLING HIM.